Witch Book

The Definitive Guide to Witch Craft,

Paganism and Everyday Magic

Glinda Abraham

© 2019

COPYRIGHT

Witch Book: The Definitive Guide to Witch Craft, Paganism and Everyday Magic

By Glinda Abraham

Copyright @2018 By Glinda Abraham

All Rights Reserved.

The following eBook is reproduced below with the goal of providing information that is as accurate and as reliable as possible. Regardless, purchasing this eBook can be seen as consent to the fact that both the publisher and the author of this book are in no way experts on the topics discussed within, and that any recommendations or suggestions made herein are for entertainment purposes only. Professionals should be consulted as needed before undertaking any of the action endorsed herein.

This declaration is deemed fair and valid by both the American Bar Association and the Committee of Publishers Association and is legally binding throughout the United States.

Furthermore, the transmission, duplication or reproduction of any of the following work, including precise information, will be considered an illegal act, irrespective whether it is done electronically or in print. The legality extends to creating a secondary or tertiary copy of the work or a recorded copy and is only allowed with express written consent of the Publisher. All additional rights are reserved.

The information in the following pages is broadly considered to be a truthful and accurate account of facts, and as such any inattention, use or misuse of the information in question by the reader will render any resulting actions solely under their purview. There are no scenarios in which the publisher or the original author of this work can be in any fashion deemed liable for any hardship or damages that may befall them after undertaking information described herein.

Additionally, the information found on the following pages is intended for informational purposes only and should thus be considered, universal. As befitting its nature, the information presented is without assurance regarding its continued validity or interim quality. Trademarks that mentioned are done without written consent and can in no way be considered an endorsement from the trademark holder.

Table of Contents

INTRODUCTION 1
    If this book came your way... 1

PART 1: PAGANISM 8
    Chapter 1: What Paganism Isn't 8
    Chapter 2: The History of Paganism 15
    Chapter 3: Paganism Today 59
    Chapter 4: How Do You Know You're a Pagan 73

PART 2: WICCA 79
    Chapter 1: Wicca Then and Now 79
    Chapter 2: What Wicca Isn't... And What It Can Be 96
    Chapter 3: Are You a Wiccan or a Witch? 105

PART 3: EVERYDAY MAGICK 120

CHAPTER 1: BASIC TOOLS AND RITUALS 120

CHAPTER 2: FIND YOUR WITCHY FLAVOR 153

CHAPTER 3: DIVINATION 101 158

CHAPTER 4: SEASONAL SPELLS 244

CHAPTER 5: FINAL WORDS OF WARNING 252

BIBLIOGRAPHY 258

INTRODUCTION

IF THIS BOOK CAME YOUR WAY…

…Then it must be for a reason.

Perhaps you always felt a close connection to Nature and her elements, a connection you couldn't quite put into proper words. All you know is that you feel most like yourself when you're out into the deep woods or by the open sea; when you can smell the rain in autumn or see the flames dance on a winter night. All you know is that there's a secret rhythm to the changing of the seasons, the phases of the Moon and the way the light fluctuates; a rhythm that you can dance to. You don't even have to know the steps.

This book is for you.

Perhaps, like so many of us, you grew up in a Christian family... but always struggled to connect. Not with Christianity's core message of love and forgiveness which is absolutely fine, but with its mainstream, religious rules and teachings. (So many things to feel bad about and repent for! Surely, we've been brought to this Earth to play, learn and have fun?) But your struggles haven't made you secular or worse, cynical. You're still looking for something to believe in, something bigger than you. Something that allows you to be your true, whole self.

Yes, dear one, this book is for you too.

Perhaps you've started walking your Pagan path already. Slowly but surely, you're soaking up every occult thing you come across. And there are so many occult things to come across in this day and age! You've bought some cute crystals at Etsy, followed a couple of witchy accounts on Instagram for inspiration and was thinking of getting your first deck of tarot cards. You're still unsure what it all means though; how it all fits together. You know you're interested in the spiritual... but can you call yourself a witch yet?

Sister, this book is definitely for you!

On the other hand, perhaps you've been on this Path for a while now. Perhaps your momma or your nanna have been teaching you rituals and spells ever since you were a little one… Perhaps these brilliant women, in their wisdom and love for you, never even called them "spells": just some movements to do, some words to say or herbs to brew when you want to help ease a loved one's pain, help your flowers grow and have prosperity at home… You have a lot of practical knowledge and skills that stem from family lore but you haven't felt the need to dive into the theoretical part of it yet.

You'll be pleased to know: this book is for you as well.

Merry meet, one and all.

In [Book Title TBD] we won't be taking any sides. We'll discuss both the Light and the Sacred Night; both the Yin and the Yang; both the theory and the practical, everyday aspects of the Path. We'll offer insights into what it means to be a Pagan, a Wiccan and a Witch — and how you can be either… or all three.

In this book, we'll talk about the past and how the journey of magick started.

We'll talk about the present and how magick is once again awakening all around us (you've felt it too, haven't you?).

And we'll talk about the future. The Earth's future but you own future too, no matter where you're coming from. We'll talk about how your magick can and will change your life, if you let it.

Throughout this book, you'll notice that as the seasons, so will our tone change. Sometimes we'll be serious: we'll warn you about all the things that could go wrong with a spell or a magical object. Other times, we'll be as lighthearted as a robin singing his song on a Spring morning. We'll urge you to not take yourself and your craft very seriously.

Nature and Magick are never just one thing — they keep changing, evolving and adapting. So will this book. So will you, in your Path. And later on, when you return to this book to reread a spell or brush up on a ritual for a Pagan holiday that's fast approaching, perhaps you'll notice things you didn't notice the first time around; you'll spot little details that escaped you, or see things you've tried for yourself and would now do a bit differently.

That's how it should be.

Your only authority on your Path, at the end of the day, is you.

We're just here to show you the way.

The way back to our ancestors and their lost, ancient teachings — but also the way forward. So that you can use that knowledge in a modern context and understand the unique blessings and struggles of this digital era we're living in.

Because although some things are much better now (hey, we're not getting burned at the stake anymore, for one) other things have also become a lot more complicated. Surely, our Pagan forefathers and foremothers never had to deal with things like "protecting your aura from electronic fields" or "struggling to align with Nature when you live in a crowded city"...

But worry not. At the end of this book, you'll have all the answers you need. At least, all the answers you need in order to start asking the real, magickal questions — the ones only you, your familiars, your matron/patron deities and your guiding spirits can answer.

The first part of this book is about Paganism.

We'll talk about what Paganism isn't (because people, throughout the ages, have had so many misconceptions about it!) and what it really is. We'll explore its rich history and its diverse present, all the way from 35,000 BCE to today. We'll see how Pagans have been exalted, hunted and burned at the stake, tolerated and then exalted again as the Wheel turns. At the end of the first part of the book, we'll go through all the things that make or break a Pagan, so that you can decide what applies to you.

The second part of this book is about Wicca.

Once again, we'll talk about what Wicca isn't (hint: it's not the same thing as Paganism, as many outsiders believe) and what Wicca really is. We'll take a look at how it started and how it has evolved to this day; we'll go through the most important Wiccan rituals and beliefs. By the end of the second part of the book, you'll know if Wicca is for you.

The third part of this book is about you.

Yes, you.

You who may or may not belong to the other two categories. You who may have a penchant for herbal magic, a knack for predictions of the future or a sixth sense when it comes to communicating with spirits. No matter what your unique gift (or gifts), we'll talk about ways to hone it; to do and be better, every day.

Yes, there will be spells. Use them wisely.

There will be tarot cards. We'll talk in as much detail as we can about what they symbolize and how they can help you in your divination practice as well as your wellness and self care rituals.

There will also be ingredients for you to create your unique blend of magick; instructions on how to manifest the energies you most desire in your life; insights on how to use other divination tools like runes or numerology without second guessing yourself; suggestions on how to celebrate Pagan holidays.

If this book came your way, then there must be a reason.

It's time for you to start reading and find out what that reason was.

PART 1: PAGANISM

CHAPTER 1: WHAT PAGANISM ISN'T

"History is written by the victors."

This is a famous saying by Winston Churchill who, while definitely not a Pagan or otherwise connected to the teachings of this book, certainly knew a thing or two about shaping narratives for political gain. "History is written by the victors" means that the winners of any conflict, be it military, monetary or social, are the ones who get to tell the story from their point of view; the ones who get to define what the "truth" is.

How is this relevant to a book about Paganism and magic, you ask?

Oh, it's very simple: when it comes to the prevailing of religions and the power they hold in society, Paganism has unfortunately lost. It took many centuries: Paganism started losing ground around the 4th century CE, and was almost completely wiped out within the following centuries in Europe. (The timeline was a bit different for other continents, with the Americas and Africa maintaining their Pagan traditions for longer, until the so called "Age of Discovery" and with the Arabic part of Asia being Islamized around the 7th century CE.)

Many people remained Pagan, sure, but they did so in secret; in fear of punishment, torture, even death if their secret came out. Punishment inflicted by the practitioners of the winning religions, the ones whose traditions were now considered the norm.

And the winners of that particular conflict were the practitioners of Christianity.

So, Christianity has gotten to define history. Even if in many an occasion, "defining" history meant blatantly distorting it; even if it meant spouting lies about what once was the dominant faith of the people or appropriating traditions as the victors saw fit.

This is not an exaggeration, it's simple facts. If you're doubting what you just read, or simply never thought of Christianity as the "victors" in a conflict that shaped history and reality itself, ask yourself this question: What year is it?

Is it, perhaps, 2019?

If you live in the Western world, the answer is yes.

But 2019 years since what?

What event is globally considered so important that has defined even the way we measure time itself? That has divided the flow of history in "Before" and "After"?

(Hint: it's someone's birthday.)

Perhaps you're starting to get it now?

Christianity has won — and because of that, history has been rewritten.

Because of that, even now, when you call yourself a Pagan openly, most people will feel unsettled (even if they're polite and will do a good job hiding it). Because of that, even now, the word Pagan is somehow associated with things dirty, wrong or unholy. Despite the fact that, by the very definition of the word, being "a Pagan" is literally the most natural thing any human being can be.

That's why the first thing we need to talk about in this book, **is what Paganism isn't.**

To clear any misconceptions people (even you!) may still be carrying deep inside, perhaps without even realizing. And to arm you with the arguments you'll need, next time you come across someone who feels offended, frightened or just unsettled by the mere word "Pagan".

Are you ready? Let's begin setting history straight, shall we?

PAGANISM IS NOT ABOUT WORSHIPING THE DEVIL

This is a long story that will make much more sense once we delve into the origins of Paganism in the next chapter. But for now, all you need to know is this: Paganism is as further away from devil worshiping and satanism as can be. In fact, Modern Satanism, is (by its own definition) deeply a-spiritual and secular so once again the opposite of what Paganism is.

Let's repeat it once more: Pagans don't worship the devil. Never had, never will. Why? Because they don't believe the devil exists — not in the sense most people think of the devil, that of the antagonist of God and master of all evil, anyway. That devil is a Christian invention.

Certainly, the idea of an absolute evil that antagonizes the absolute good can be found in many religions. But the idea that Pagans worship the devil/absolute evil, is basically propaganda created in the early years of Christianity, to scare people away from Paganism.

Yes, many Pagan gods, deities and creatures of Pagan lore have horns. But so do goats. Are goats evil? The mere idea is laughable, isn't it? And yet, any depictions of horned Pagan deities (like the Greek god Pan, satyrs or fauns) have been reinterpreted by Christianity as diabolical...

We'll get more in depth into the how and why that happened, in the next chapter.

Paganism is not location specific

Every single civilization on Earth has its own Pagan traditions. Although when we say the word "Pagan" most of us think in European/Western World terms, the truth is that the Pagan traditions of Native Americans, Africans and Aboriginal Australians are by no means any less rich or important than their European counterparts. (If anything, they're probably richer because they had more time to grow roots in people's consciousness, as Christianity reached these places much later than it did Europe.)

That's why Paganism today is such a diverse practice: every practitioner carries his or her own local traditions and there is an endless well of knowledge to tap into.

Now, isn't that beautiful?

PAGANISM IS NOT THE ENEMY OF CHRISTIANITY — OR ANY RELIGION, REALLY

Being a Pagan doesn't make you hate Christians. (Although for many years, the exact opposite could have been said to be true.)

More importantly, Paganism is not a religion: at least not one, single religion, with common characteristics among its practitioners and a well-defined dogma as most organized religions are. The Pagan mindset, although not always polytheistic (since every place has its own traditions), is fundamentally about accepting and understanding that there are many forces out there: there shouldn't be one single authority to overrule them all.

Today, you'll see many Pagans also embracing Christian, Jewish or Buddhist traditions. That's because they know we are all children of Nature and are all, at the end of the day, talking about the same thing in different words. For a true Pagan, there are no victors and losers: life is complicated and circular — and what goes around comes around.

Paganism is certainly coming back around today, isn't it?

History may be written by the victors, but myths and legends are written by the oppressed; to transfer traditions and beliefs from generations to generations, disguised as fairy tales. And when it comes to the human psyche, myths and legends are much more powerful.

CHAPTER 2: THE HISTORY OF PAGANISM

I know what you're thinking.

"History is boring. Who wants to read all that anyway? Where are the spells?"

Am I right? Are you thinking something like that?

Here's the thing, dear one.

No one is forcing you to do anything you don't want to do. No one is forcing you to read anything you don't want to read. In fact, you can skip ahead to the third part of the book, where all the practical, fun stuff await, where you'll learn how to do real spells…

But wait. I have to warn you of the consequences, if you choose to do that.

To perform any spell, even the simplest one, you need to understand and respect the forces you're working with. If you don't understand them, nothing will happen — no matter how long you chant or how many fancy ingredients you've gathered. If you don't respect them... well, then you're risking angering some of them and inviting serious repercussions in your life.

(I've seen first-hand what happens when people try to cast love spells with no idea what they're doing or without acknowledging all the forces at play... These people only end up tying their own emotions and lives to that other person, the recipient of the spell, who still doesn't care about them. They are unable to get over that person; they spend their lives in frustration and misery. And that's just a mild example of a spell gone wrong.)

Imagine walking into a chemistry lab to perform an experiment. Would you ever do that without knowing the periodic table first? Without understanding what every element does and how they tend to interact together? Would you conduct any of your experiments without wearing gloves, a lab coat or even goggles?

Definitely not — unless you want your lab to explode.

That's why, as a Pagan, a Wiccan and a Witch, understanding your history is important. Your ancestors, the people who have walked this Path before you, have suffered a lot. They were persecuted, demonized, colonized; they had to adapt, to find inventive ways to stay true to their beliefs. That only made their magic stronger.

You're one of the lucky ones. You don't have to suffer (although sometimes, life will serve you some suffering if there are lessons to be learned and you're refusing to learn them). You just need to soak up their wisdom. To learn and understand who they were, what they've been through and how it all fits together.

That's why this history lesson is important. For your own good, please don't skip it.

The dawn of Pagan worshipping

Let's backtrack a bit. In the previous chapter, "What Paganism Isn't", we mentioned at some point that Paganism is not a religion.

Well, it isn't. At least not in the sense that we've learned to understand religions through the lens of Christianity, Jewdaism, Islam and Hinduism (and to a lesser extent, Buddhism): as set systems with a formal dogma and rules that anyone who consider themselves a believer is expected to abide to — and all those who don't are infidels that need to either be dealt with, converted or at the very least frowned upon.

If you ask historians today, paganism is more accurately defined as a sum of numerous different "cults"[1], operating without a written religious doctrine or a formal version of what is considered the "right, official way" to worship. Did each "cult" was sure their beliefs were probably more to the point than the beliefs of other "cults"? Yes, probably. Did they go to war about it? Not really. Of course there was fighting and wars in the Pagan world; brutal wars in fact. We're not here to claim that Pagans were all peace-loving people. But spreading one's deities to another region was never very high among the reasons two clans or kingdoms would fight each other.

There's a simple reason for that: ancient Pagans understood that no god or goddess on their own could be the ultimate source of authority over everything and everyone. They accepted contrasting forces, within Nature as well as within their belief systems — that's why it was easier for them to accept other people's beliefs. Even if, in many occasions, they would make fun of each other's gods (or believe that a war would be won because their gods were ultimately stronger than those of their opponents).

---

[1] Cameron, Alan G. (2011). The Last Pagans of Rome. New York: Oxford University Press, p. 26-27

Another reason is the lack of organization that comes from having a formal creed. There were sacred texts, certainly, but Pagan beliefs were mostly spread through word of mouth; through the tales the elders would tell the young while gathered around the fire, the rain storming outside. Myth, legend and folklore were intertwined (and often indistinguishable) with stories about how the world and the gods came to be. And along with the person who would do the retelling every time, the story would change slightly.

That doesn't mean Pagan beliefs are a collection of fables. At least not in the sense you think of fables today as something "not true". But they were certainly more dynamic and less "set in stone" than the beliefs of the dominant religions of today.

Why? Well, you need to consider the time all this happened.

We did say this would be a bit of a history lesson, didn't we?

Paganism predates the written word. In fact it wouldn't be wrong to say that Paganism, in its various expressions depending on the corner of the globe you look at, has been the first spirituality system humanity ever came up with.

Now, notice how we said "they first spirituality system" and not "the first religion"?

Historians, anthropologists and religious researchers alike have been trying forever to pinpoint what was "the first religion" known to man — some of them for historical purposes, others with the motive to prove that their own religion was the first, ergo, the "original" one. But here's the thing: human evolution doesn't exactly work that way. Same was as it is now proven that there was not one single "cradle of civilization" from which we all emerged, there was never one single "original religion" as well.

When humanity was still relatively new to this planet (and there weren't so many of us around) we were probably more similar to one another than ever. We all faced the same threats to our survival: wild animals that could hunt and kill us if we strayed too far from the fire, harsh winters that made it impossible to find food, droughts that made our crops die, diseases that ravaged us from an early age making it necessary to have a strong body and do everything as young as possible... It wasn't very easy being human back then, was it?

No, it wasn't. We needed help to get by. To make sure our crops would survive, our children would grow up strong and our fire wouldn't die out in the middle of the night. So we looked for help in the only places we knew: the magnificence of Nature — and the support of one another.

We developed our own explanations for natural phenomena: the changing of the seasons, the sudden burst of lightning, the winds that sometimes wouldn't come when we wanted our ships to sail. In awe of Nature and her manifestations that were so much more powerful than us, we came up with names and backstories for all these supernatural entities that were clearly all around us; for all these forces of Nature that could save or ruin our lives.

And guess what? The names of these deities may have been different from one another, depending on what part of the world you were in, but their essense wasn't. It doesn't matter if she was called Aphrodite, Venus, Freya, Oshun or Xochiquetzal: people believed in a goddess that protected love, lust, childbirth and women. Almost every Pagan culture has a goddess of fertility, a goddess of home and a goddess of love (very often, the three are one and the same); a god of the sun and a god or goddess of the underworld; a god of war and a god or goddess of wisdom. These gods and goddesses were believed to interact with one another the way forces of Nature do: sometimes favorably, other times causing chaos.

Let's hop on a time machine and examine a bit more how it all started, shall we?

The year was 35,000 BCE.

We still mostly lived in caves, but we'd mastered the art of moving around in boats, as well as the art of using plants for healing. We lived in small communities in what was back then Eurasia and venerated the circle of life, from birth to death. Archaeological finds from that era up until 26,000 BCE, show burials of bones stained with red ochre, which most of them agree it likely was for spiritual purposes. Red ochre symbolized the body being returned to Mother Earth, the Great Goddess — and entering the circle of rebirth through blood.

Already back then, the Divine Feminine was present in the human psyche. That's when the first "Venus figurines" first started appearing in graves all across Eurasia[2].

Yes, you got that right: the first recurring artifact to be found across all human civilization, was not a depiction of power and war (like Zeus' lightning bolt or Thor's hammer) or of exalted wisdom (like the Star of David) or even of sacrifice and martyrdom (like the Christian cross). It was one that revered the female form and celebrated life and fertility. Carved from stone, ivory or formed in clay, these Venus figurines all had large breasts, full bellies and hips

---

[2] Dixson, Alan F., and Barnaby Dixson. 2011. "Venus Figurines of the European Paleolithic: Symbols of Fertility or Attractiveness?" Journal of Anthropology 2011, p. 1-11.

and exposed vulvas. Although modern historians are still not 100% in agreement as per the exact purpose of these figurines, the general consensus is that they were probably emblems of fertility, success and the Mother Goddess.

Isn't it interesting that our first statues, collectively as a species, celebrated Nature and honored life through the female form?

It makes sense, if you think about it. What was Earth, back then, if not the Great Mother who nurtured us all and provided us with food and warmth to survive?

Of course, Earth still is the Great Mother. She hasn't changed. It's us who changed a lot throughout the millennia, to the point that we forgot we owe everything to Her; to the point that today we think we could deplete her resources completely and then hop on to a spaceship and colonize some other unfortunate planet...

But let's not get carried away yet! We still have a lot of ground to cover in this trip through time.

From about 10,000 BCE to 100 BCE, different ancient civilizations flourished.

And their diverse Pagan traditions flourished with them.

Humanity's oldest temple (that we've discovered so far) is believed to have been in use between 9,000 BCE and 7,000 BCE, in the

Southeastern Anatolia Region of Turkey. It's called "Göbekli Tepe" which is Turkish for "potbelly hill" and is thought to be a pilgrimage site where people honored Nature and its creatures (pillar carvings of various animals as well as people have been found there). It's also thought that the site functioned as a cosmogonic map of sorts, for the locals to understand how they were all connected — both to the landscape that surrounded them and to the cosmos. The archaeologist behind this discovery believes that the people who built Göbekli Tepe were practicing shamanism and worshipped deities that were much later found in ancient Mesopotamia…

A millennia or so later, again in Anatolia, at the proto-city settlements of Catalhoyuk, people seemed to use figurines that once again exalted the feminine body — only this time, there were also phallic symbols and hunting scenes. Mother Nature was still at the core of spiritual beliefs, but powerful individual expressions of her (like the sun or the mountains) were slowly emerging as manifestations of male deities.

You can see the common theme, right?

It was all about the embodiment of Nature in physical structures and forms: female and male; human and divine. We'd started mapping not just our inner duality but also our relationship to the animals, the stars and the cosmos.

And this was not only the case in Turkey, but all across the other side of Europe as well.

Around 3,000 BCE, some of the most intriguing structures started appearing in Ireland and what is now the United Kingdom. The first one, Newgrange, was a huge circular tomb, tightly surrounded by a stoned circle (almost like a crown would surround a king's head). It has carvings from rose quartz and is positioned in such a way that, when the Sun rising on the day of the Winter Solstice, its rays hit directly the tomb's entrance and flood the inner chamber with light. Winter Solstice in general, was one of the most important times of the year for Pagans: when the longest night of the year was over, and there was once again hope for spring and renewal. The walls of Newgrange are adorned with spirals; a symbol of renewal and eternity. It was believed that gods resided inside! Although archaeologists cannot agree on why Newgrange was built (do they ever agree on anything?), the two most possible explanations are that it was either part of a religion that venerated the Sun and how it moved in the sky, or the dead and their passage to underworld. If you take into account the dualities we've already seen in earlier temples, it was probably both: a celebration of like (the Sun) and death (the Underworld). We'll see something similar when we talk about the pyramids in a while.

Newgrange certainly wasn't the only structure in that corner of the world that was built perfectly aligned with a solstice or an equinox... You may know one of these other structures.

It's Stonehenge.

Stonehenge was initially built around 3,100 BCE — although it continued evolving until 2,600 BCE. A wooden circle is thought to have originally existed within the stone circle, with the wooden posts later replaced with its current standing stones. Although the stone circles look rather abstract and minimal today, back then its architecture was quite complex: it had an altar, a cremation cemetery, a portal and subtle engravings on its stones show symbols like a dagger and an ax. To this day, no one knows how its builders managed to move the huge monoliths around, but we do know that they made sure they were perfectly aligned with the midsummer sunrise and the midwinter sunset of that time.

Stonehenge is considered to be a place of immense power. It's no accident that the ancients built their temples in the places they did, perfectly aligned with the elements of Nature. It is believed that they followed invisible "ley lines", energy lines from within the

Earth that made some locations more magically potent than others[3]. That belief was especially strong among the Celtic Druids — and it's something many modern Pagans believe to this day.

But let's get back to our time machine, this time to visit ancient Egypt and the Pyramids.

Ah, the Pyramids! One could write a whole book about the Pyramids and still not manage to scratch the surface of their complex spiritual importance… but we can at least try to figure out how it all fits together in this ancient Pagan puzzle, can't we?

Around 2,635 BCE, the oldest surviving Pyramid was commissioned by a Pharaoh and started its construction. One hundred years later, the Great Pyramid of Giza had been completed — and a hundred years after that, around 2,494 BCE, the Pyramid Texts were composed; one of the oldest religious texts that have survived to this day. This marks an era when Paganism, at least in the more developed parts of the ancient world, was beginning to acquire a more well-defined shape. This is roughly around the time when the first pantheons started appearing; different gods and

---

[3] Doyle White, Ethan (2016). "Old Stones, New Rites: Contemporary Pagan Interactions with the Medway Megaliths". Material Religion: The Journal of Objects, Art and Belief, p. 346-372.

goddesses, each "responsible" for a specific domain of Nature and human life. These pantheons are first encountered in Mesopotamia, Egypt and Greece, but later become common among Pagan religions in China, South America and Africa as well.

You could almost say that what started with simply worshipping Mother Nature, evolved to worshipping some of its manifestations… to worshipping the different conditions of human life. There are several common threads throughout these pantheons, that we've briefly touched before and will discuss more in a later chapter. Because we're not done with the Pyramids yet!

The Pyramids are perhaps the best example of the duality of Paganism: combining the worship of the Sun and its light, with the veneration for the dead and their shadow kingdom. They were all built on the west side of the Nile, which was considered the domain of the dead and were given names that were all somehow associated with the light of the Sun. The structures themselves speak to that underlying duality, with their broad base that reached under the earth and their pointy edge towards the sky… The idea is the same as the idea behind a witch's conical hat really: to create a cone of power. Some believe that the power was so strong that the pyramids were designed as a resurrection "machine" for the Pharaohs to come back to life!

Now wouldn't that make a much more interesting movie than all those mummy horror films?

Speaking of fascinating stories that are not being told often enough: the Minoan civilization. Established around 2,200 BCE in ancient Crete, with its epicenter at Knossos palace, the Minoan civilization was actually considered the first advanced society in Europe. Now you may have heard the tale of the Minotaur, the mythical half-man, half-bull monster that lived inside the maze… but did you know that the Minoan civilization was fundamentally matriarchal, with women in equal positions as men, very often being naked from the waste up like men?

Yes, naked female breasts in ancient Crete were not a taboo[4] as they seem to be in today's Instagram… And this has its roots in the Pagan mentality of viewing the woman body as something to be celebrated and aspired to; something strong and primal not delicate and hidden away in shame. In fact the most important goddess of the Minoans, the goddess of the snakes (who is believed to be an earlier version of goddess Athena) is always posing proud in figurines, with her breasts uncovered while otherwise dressed in an exquisite gown, one snake in each arm. Why snakes? They were

---

[4] Nikos Kazantzakis. At the Palaces of Knossos. London: Owen, 1988.

always a symbol of wisdom, but also of change and rebirth; of shedding one's skin. (We'll elaborate more on Pagan and magical symbols on a later chapter.)

But to get back to the pyramids for one last time: Egyptians were not the only ones who built them. Around 1,200 BCE, the Olmecs in Central America started building pyramids too — once again to venerate the dead. Later on, around 250–900 CE, the Mayan pyramids were built...

Isn't it fascinating to see how, in such ancient times, humanity was pretty much in agreement about the truly important things in life? Not sameness, as each culture gave its own spin on things, but an agreement nonetheless. Modern humans could definitely stand to learn a thing or two from ancient Pagans in that regard (and many others).

Next stop on our journey: the first sparks of monotheism appear around the world.

And guess what? It coincides with the first versions of written creed...

From 2,150 until about 600 BCE, sacred scripture are beginning to emerge throughout the known civilization. First in Sumeria, with the Epic of Gilgamesh, a king chosen by the gods to save his people, who along the way spurned the gods and learned the secrets to immortality. Then in India, around 1,700 BCE, the first one of the Vedas (the oldest scriptures of Hinduism) was composed; it talked, among other things, about a supreme god. This kickstarted the Vedic age, the formative period of the Indian civilization. Around 1,250 BCE, the Upanishads were composed: these later Vedic texts contain some of the central concepts that then evolved to Hinduism and Buddhism.

Then, around 600 BCE, the Torah was compiled. Torah was the first of the sacred Jewish books that created the Hebrew bible: they spoke about how the Jewish were god's chosen people and they had to endure a lot of suffering and live by certain strict laws. It was believed that the teachings of the Torah were given to the prophet Moses directly by Yahweh, the god of the Jews (that later evolved to the God of Christianity) and he wrote them down.

Around the same era, a bit further away, the emperors Darius and Xerxes are making Zoroastrianism the official religion of their expanding Persian empire. Zoroastrianism was all about the fight between the absolute good, a supreme god called Ahura Mazda ("Wise Lord" in Iranian) and absolute evil, as preached by the spiritual leader Zaratustra.

Confucius in China also compiled his first book during that same time. Shu Ching, written in the form of speeches from a king to his ministers, discussed ideas about the morality of government, venerating the ancestors and not doing to others what you don't want others doing to you[5]… (A lovely message, to this day.) A hundred years or so after that, Buddha was born.

It would be another 400 years or so until the birth of Jesus Christ…

MAKING THE WORLD A MORE MONOTHEISTIC PLACE

Well, that was a looong trip through time, wasn't it? You practically witnessed the dawn of spirituality and religion in fast forward within a few minutes… It's okay if your head is spinning!

Take a few moments to breathe.

It's now time to unpack all these things we just learned and understand them a bit better, in terms of how they affected Pagan beliefs and the way the world works today.

Basically it can be condensed into one sentence: as people moved further away from Nature, building intricate cities and creating laws where the will of the king had to be venerated, monotheism started taking over. And in every single case, the ultimate god was considered to have male characteristics (not in the sense of having a

---

[5] Medhurst, W. H. Ancient China. The Shoo King or the Historical Classic. Shanghai: The Mission Press.

male body, but in the sense of propagating male, patriarchal values).

Was that an accident? Not really! The kings and emperors of ancient civilizations (with the exception of Classical Greece that had already invented democracy by then), were men, following a bloodline that was believed to have been blessed by the gods. So they needed an ultimate "overruler", an authority that could bypass all others and that people would obey.

That authority, normally, it had to look a bit like them.

So you go from a place in the collective human psyche where the female form is venerated as a manifestation of Mother Earth and the Primordial Goddess, to a place where man-made texts and laws are considered to contain the only truth. A truth that, conveniently, always involves a male-like being, usually older and wise, ruling over everyone — sometimes benevolently, others through fear.

Can you see what's happening here? We went from honoring Nature the notion that we are made of nature and should live in alignment to that nature (cue all those buildings aligned with the rays of the sun), to believing we are somehow greater than Nature and that we should live in alignment to a divine wisdom (even if we have to suffer or follow strict rules). It's a fundamental shift, the repercussions of which we are experiencing to this day. Because what is blatant capitalism and the burning of the Amazon's rainforests for profit if not the evolution of the monotheistic idea that we are somehow "better", "chosen" and that we "deserve" to take everything we want since our way is the only correct way?

Just think for a second how the Bible starts: "In the beginning was the Word, and the Word was with God, and the Word was God[6]."

If you honestly believe that a superior, male-presenting wisdom created Nature, then you're going to lead a very different life than those who believe that Nature IS the superior wisdom. If you think that wisdom and male authority trumps female power and the miracle of childbirth, then you're going to have a very different society than the ancient Minoans where women had their breasts uncovered. If you believe that one god is all you need, then you'll have a very different way of managing disputes and expanding your kingdom than the ancient Greeks who had 12 gods (6 male, 6 female) and even saw monarchy as something that could be debated — at least until Alexander the Great came along.

Of course, the counterargument can also be made: didn't these empires flourish as much as they did precisely BECAUSE they believed their one and only god told them to march on? Because they had explicit laws and rules and sacred scriptures instead of relying on an oral tradition and more or less only fighting each other for resources? Isn't this the reason polytheistic societies like

---

[6] Old Testament: The Book of Genesis.

those of the native Americans and Africans fell prey to the European colonizers who believed they were on a sacred mission to christianize the world? Didn't organize religion also bring about a society that was able to expand exponentially?

Probably. But this is not a book about how to best colonize the world or rule over your fellow humans. There have been enough books like that, written throughout the ages. As a species, we're not that much better off for it — especially if you were unlucky enough to be born in the areas of the world that were colonized, looted and enslaved by these "wise" believers in monotheism who brought their "civilization to the primitive world".

This is a book about understanding where we all came from: the womb of the same Mother Earth. Whether we've turned our backs at it or not, Paganism is a part of our psyche. Our bodies are still a manifestation of dualities. Childbirth is still a miracle. And the appreciation of feminine power is finally returning.

Dear one, this is a book to help you understand that what you believe, shapes your world.

And for a very long time, our world has been shaped by people who have turned their backs to our Pagan past and to our common, Mother Earth.

It's time to take our world back, don't you think?

But first, let's talk a bit about how the word "Pagan" came to be.

"They are crazy, these Romans⁷"

Have you noticed something from our trip through time? The word "Pagan" was never used by the ancient people to define themselves and their beliefs.

That's because that word didn't even exist yet: it was first coined around 300 CE.

Incidentally (just kidding, it wasn't incidentally at all), that was the time when the ruler of most of the then known world, the Roman Empire under the emperor Constantine, declared Christianity as its official religion.

There are many reasons why that happened, depending on who you ask.

The main (read: Christian) narrative says that in the decades that followed the death of Christ, the work of the Apostle Paul and his letters reached people in every corner of the Roman Empire, creating pockets of early Christianity. Although Christianity was

---

[7] English translation of the phrase, « Ils sont fous, ces Romains ! » from the comic book Astérix by René Goscinny and Albert Uderzo, first mentioned in Astérix et Cléopâtre, p. 10, p. 23.

persecuted and illegal, secret Chrstian societies started growing despite their very often violent deaths in Roman arena, torn asunder by lions... Christians suffered, but it only made their faith stronger — until the emperor Constantine saw the light and converted to Christianity himself.

We've all seen this movie, haven't we? Some variation of it always plays on TV around Easter...

As always, the truth is slightly more complicated.

The Romans didn't care so much about Christians per se. Judaism was a formal religion under the Roman Empire — as it was easier for the Romans to control larger territories if they allowed their subjects to keep their ways and customs. So unless Christians did something to challenge Roman authority (or were accused of doing so by someone who had a bias against them for personal reasons), they were mostly left alone.

Yes, Romans were a bloodthirsty bunch and people were thrown to the lions in the arena, there's no denying that. But it wasn't just Christians who suffered this horrible fate: it was basically everyone who would break the Roman law and wasn't highborn enough to be granted a more dignified death like beheading.

Around 200 CE, emperor Decius believed that the Roman Empire needed to strengthen its roots to avoid infighting and present a united front to the many threats they were facing (like the Goths). So he made sacrificing to the Roman gods a law of the Empire — as well as providing proof of having sacrificed to the gods. This led to many Christians who lived under Roman rule to not be able to comply… and as a result become persecuted. Interestingly enough, Decius' ruling of "mandatory sacrifice" didn't do much to stop the Goths from winning battles against the Romans. He himself died in battle.

Around 300 CE, emperor Constantine tried a different approach. Not only he granted Christianity a legal status and stopped the persecutions, he eventually declared it the official religion of the Roman Empire. The thing is though, historians today are still not sure if Constantine's motives were sincere or political: there was something about that new Christian religion, that unwavering belief that comes from monotheism, that just seemed to organize people better under a cause than it did the (by then used to a luxurious and hedonistic lifestyle) Romans who still worshipped the Roman pantheon. There are many sources that claim Constantine used Christianity as a way to promote obedience to his imperialistic policies, turning the figurehead of the emperor to that of someone who's executing God's will on Earth — and that he remained secretly Pagan until he was baptized on his deathbed.

We've all seen enough *Game of Thrones* episodes to know this is not unlikely.

In any case, it was under Constantine's rule that Christianity first became a source of power and authority. Of course, it wasn't an easy task to pull off, convincing the Romans to give up their gods and goddesses. That's where the word "Pagan" comes in.

For the first time ever, a word was needed to describe all those who haven't converted to Christianity and still believed in the old gods and goddesses. That word had to be inclusive enough so as to capture all the different beliefs that fell under the would-be-Pagan umbrella, but also subtly derogatory to make it clear that Christians were now the first-class citizens.

Words like "hellene" (to signify those who worshipped the Greek-Roman pantheon) and "heathen" (meaning the one who dwells on the heath) started being used. But "Pagan", from the Latin word for "rural/rustic/villager/relating to the countryside/non-military" (paganus), seemed like the perfect fit — and eventually became interchangeable with "non-Christian". Why?

If you understand Constantine's reasons for the official switch to Christianity as a way to "rally the troops", then it's easy to see how people who still opted to practice the old religions started feeling ostracized. It became easier for them to start living a more rural life that didn't get them in the crosshairs of the now-Christian population that lived in the more urban areas; living closer to nature where they could practice their beliefs in peace made sense. Another reason is that according to Constantine's imperialistic vision, all Christians were considered "milites Christi": soldiers of Christ (and of the Roman Empire, it goes without saying).

It bears repeating, dear one: Pagans didn't choose the word "pagan" to describe themselves. It was a derogatory term applied to them by those in power — fueled by political propaganda and propagated by ignorance. Not unsimilar to the way the name "Indians" was given to native Americans by the colonizers (first by mistake, then to signify their inferiority to Europeans).

History is written by the victors, didn't we establish that?

Of course, the same way Rome "wasn't built in a day", so Christianity didn't take over the Roman Empire completely overnight. And although the now-called Pagans certainly didn't feel like they had more in common between them than before (for instance, a Norse Pagan would never consider themselves of the same tribe with a Celtic Pagan or a Greek Pagan), slowly they started realizing that living under Christian rule meant they would either have to hide themselves, or rebel and suffer the consequences.

Many of them chose the latter — while others practiced their craft in secret, "hiding" Pagan symbols in everything from actual Christian churches to little home decorations.

They didn't always have to hide their symbols though. In a bizarre twist of fate, many Pagan symbols and traditions were actually incorporated into canon Christianity. Especially when it came to Christmas. Many Germanic/Scandinavian and Celtic rituals and symbols, from kissing under the mistletoe (a holy plant in both Scandinavian and Celtic lore) to burning the Yule log (a Norse Winter Solstice tradition) and even decorating fyr trees with lights and presents (another Norse tradition, to honor Odin) were eventually incorporated into Christmas celebrations. But that happened a bit later.

For now all you need to know is that the date of Christmas itself, we owe to Pagans. Yes, really.

It was during those early days, when the Church had to convince people to give up their Pagan ways and join the reinvented, all-Christian Roman Empire. Suffice to say it wasn't easy, especially when it came to the bon viveur Romans. Romans liked their parties and never missed an opportunity to celebrate. For instance: upon the Winter Solstice, which as we've seen was a big deal for all Pagans, the Romans and Greeks traditionally celebrated Saturnalia — the birth of Saturn/Kronos.

Originally celebrated on December 17, the birth of Saturn was a week-long, lavish celebration where people would roam the streets sans clothing, carol singing, binge drinking and exchanging gifts. Shops and businesses would close, food and drink would be aplenty... There was no easy way to convince a whole nation to forego a party like that, especially when that nation was the Romans! So the Church declared the birth of Christ to be celebrated on December 25 and made it "8 days of Christmas" — so that people could start celebrating on the 17th as they were used to. Brilliant, right? It was that "8 days of Christmas" that slowly evolved to the "12 days of Christmas" of today.

And transferring Christmas in December (we say "transferring" because most historians now believe Christ was born in the Spring) didn't just placate the Romans[8]. It helped the Zoroastrians adapt as well, as the birth of Mithra, who was also called "The Invincible Sun" took place on December 25. And of course it fit all the other Pagan cultures who viewed the Winter Solstice as a day of hope and love, where the Light is reborn....

---

[8] William Walsh, The Story of Santa Klaus, 1970, p. 62.

Hey, nothing wrong with that. A new religion comes along and incorporates rituals, symbols and beliefs from the old religions to keep people happy. It's a good thing, right?

Unfortunately, it didn't stop there.

As many people back in the day tended to combine their newfound Christianity with many of their Pagan practices (like sacrifices, divination, Pagan festivals, believing in omens etc), the Church needed to draw a line in the sand, of sorts. They needed to convince people that the Pagan ways were wrong and evil, instead of what they really were at the time, aka politically inconvenient. And the way to do that was by taking some key Pagan practices and symbols and vilifying them.

To get back to the misconceptions about Paganism discussed on the first chapter: the reason people have this idea that Pagans worship the devil, is because the Church took some of Paganism's most popular deities and use their physical characteristics to create the image of the Devil; the antithesis of God; the absolute evil. Who were these deities?

Mostly Pan, the Greek god of nature and wild animals, who was depicted as half-man, half-goat, with horns sprouting from his head. Pan was never evil: he was a fun-loving being who embraced the joys of nature, virility and sex, although his temper would often cause panic (yes, that's where that word comes from) to his opponents. He was worshipped in the outdoors and was often depicted in statues and paintings with an erect member...

You can see, perhaps, why the newly founded Christian church would not like that?

Pan symbolized everything (interestingly enough "everything" is literally what the name Pan translates to in Greek) this new religion wanted to break free from: sexual freedom, a close connection to nature, a reverence of the naked body. Jesus Christ's message at its core may have been one of love and forgiveness, but the framework around Christianity was still very much influenced by Judaism (Christianity was considered the "continuation" of Judaism anyway, it is commonly accepted that both religions believe in the same God). And Judaism, as we've seen, preached piety and suffering in order to be accepted in god's kingdom after death.

Abstaining from temptation, was Christianity's main theme. And nothing was more tempting than the fun-loving gods of Pagans who preached being laissez-faire and celebrating your body and your desires, as well as your connection to the animal world...

Another such "offender" was Cernunnos, the horned god of the Celts and the Gauls. Cernunnos is depicted with antlers on his head and always surrounded by wild animals (among them stags, snakes, bulls and rats, all symbols of wisdom and virility). In contrast to Pan though, Cernunnos is peaceful, sitting calm and cross legged — something historians believe symbolized his dual nature, embracing both human wisdom and empathy and animal power, presiding over both Nature and the Underworld. Yes, those Pagan dualities again… Aren't they beautiful?

Cernunnos is worshipped today by modern Wiccans (more on that in the next part of the book).

Anyway, perhaps you're starting to get it now. Horns, a symbol of fertility and abundance, were connected with evil. Women who were free and shameless about their sexuality, were called witches (or whores, with the example of Mary Magdalene in the Bible being "saved" by Jesus and repenting for her sins). What was once a revered connection to Nature and its magnificence, the female body, started becoming a thing of shame that had to be hidden and only viewed by specific men (like a woman's husband).

Male sexuality was also stifled (there are no winners in this game of oppression). Men were supposed to only engage in "carnal relations" with their spouses with the goal to procreate, whereas homosexuality was considered a perversion and abomination…

The most heartbreaking thing? There are still people out there, so many centuries later, that still think in those terms. That are so far removed from their primordial Nature they can't see we are all unique — and perfect just the way we are.

But we should continue our journey through time, dear one.

Dark stuff happened in the Dark Ages

From about 500 CE to 1,500 CE, Europe went under what is now known as "the Dark Ages". During that time, to be accused of being a pagan (or a witch, as these terms were all piled under the same "non-devout Christian" accusation) was not just derogatory. Certainly, pagans were thought to be unclean, hedonistic, savages even — but most importantly they were considered sinners in the eyes of the One True God of Christianity. Sinners that had to either convert, or die brutal deaths. Charlemagne, king of the Franks, the Lombards and eventually emperor of the Romans, who's also called "Father Europe" because he "united and christianized the continent" personally hunted down the Pagan Saxons in order to christianize Saxonia (what is now England) chasing them on horseback on a river to give them the chance to "get baptized or die".

And we called Romans bloodthirsty a while ago when they were throwing Christians to the lions.

Around 800 CE, Pagan traditions were only practiced in secret as the official religion of the continent was for the most part Christianity. Yet, Paganism didn't die out.

The Vikings saw to that.

Also known as "the Old Norse religion", Norse paganism was practiced in Scandinavia (and among the Germanic tribes that descended through Europe) since 500 BCE. The Norse/Germanic pantheon had many similarities with the Greek/Roman pantheon: a group of gods and goddesses, closely connected to nature and to animals, none of them completely good or completely evil. Even the trickster god, Loki (who is compared to Hermes/Mercury), had moments of heroic redemption for every bad prank he pulled to the other gods[9]...

Yes, exactly like in the comics and in the superhero movies. Isn't it funny how our modern pop culture celebrates so many Pagan elements? It was about time, perhaps!

The Viking Age, from around 700 CE to 1,000 CE, brought Christianity and Pagans at a clash throughout Europe. As Scandinavians left their calm, farm lives, boarded ships and started

---

[9] Neil Gaiman, Norse Mythology, 2017, Bloomsbury Publishing PLC.

invading the European shores, they brought with them tales about Odin's wisdom, about Thor's power and Freya's beauty. They were the enemy, certainly, ransaking villages and looting churches — but form some people they were also a reminder of a different way of life; a life that was more free (and for women, certainly more equal). Christian women finding Vikings attractive and laying with them started being a frequent occurrence (with many illegitimate children born along the way) so the Church and the kings of Europe had to portray the Vikings as filthy, uncivilised animals who (you guessed it) worshipped the Devil.

Regardless, at the height of their military expansion the Vikings reached as far south as Sicily and as far West as the then unexplored America — and part of their Pagan beliefs came with them and grew roots in these new places, embedded with the local folk customs.

Remember when we talked about the Yule Log and decorating trees at Christmas earlier?

Even the myth of Santa Claus, riding his sleigh in the sky, is for the most part inspired by Odin (the AllFather of Old Norse Pantheon, often compared to Saturn or Zeus) riding his 8-legged flying horse, Sleipnir, visiting children at night and leaving gifts (or coal if they were bad) for them inside their boots. Although St Nicholas did live around 200 CE and gave a lot to the poor, as did Agios Vasileios, the Orthodox Christian version of Santa Claus around 300 CE, their figures eventually melted together with legends around Odin and his gift giving and ended up in the version of Santa Claus we have today.

(Who only started wearing red at the beginning of last century, thanks to a Coca Cola advertisement, but that's another story.)

But while West and Central Europe was discovering a unique balance of combining Pagan beliefs with a Christian official facade (to get a sense of how extended this intermingling was, just pay close attention to the symbols you'll find carved in old churches: you'll find everything from Thor's hammer there to vulva-like depictions of fruits and flowers, that echoe the symbols used to honor goddesses in many Pagan pantheons), the East was another story.

Byzantium, the continuation of the Roman Empire that became independent since the Church schism in 1054 CE, was a highly theocratic society that prosecuted viciously not just any perceived Pagans but also any different versions of Christianity (they were called heretics). Meanwhile, in the Arab world, any Pagans had converted to Islam around 700 CE.

And speaking of Islam: Paganism was not the only thing Christianity tried to stifle. Islam, back then, didn't have the militant approach many practicioners of this religion have today. On the contrary, they were probably more civilized and kind than the Europeans (and we owe a lot to Islamic scholars who translated most Ancient Greek texts and brought them to the surface once again), who launched eight Crusades to "drive the non-believers away from the Holy Land".

But that's what happens when you believe there is only one God out there; that yours is the only right one and that all others are impostors. In a way, it wasn't the Christians' fault either: they were bound to be geared like that ever since they turned monotheism into a way to control countries and armies...

Dear one, we need to jump ahead a few centuries now. And what comes next is not pleasant, not at all. But it needs to be discussed.

After all, this has been a long trip through time that's now reaching one of its most crucial moments for your understanding of what it means to be a Pagan…

It all started with a book, published in 1486 CE.

The book was called, "Malleus Maleficarum[10]".

---

[10] Malleus Maleficarum, Heinrich Kramer & Jacob Sprenger, translated by Montague Summers, 2011, Martino Fine Books.

Now, you may have noticed that we haven't really addressed witchcraft at all so far. Rest assured we will do so in the next part of the book. For now, all you need to know is that witchcraft has been around for millennia. It wasn't always considered good or bad: in many cultures, sorcerers were viewed as healers/holy people who would help with the crops and soothe illnesses. In others, sorcerers worked with kings and queens to consolidate their power and help them vanquish their enemies, the same way today modern presidents would have advisors on certain matters.

But witchcraft was also a part of everyday life. The first written mention we have of it comes from 2,000 BCE, when in the Babylonian code of law in Ancient Mesopotamia, the Code of Hammurabi[11], it is mentioned a process for a man to cleanse himself from a spell another man has cast on him by jumping into the holy river…

Notice how this was about men, not women, casting spells at each other?

Although the near Eastern antiquity has some great lore pertaining powerful female sorceresses, among them Medea (who first appears

---

[11] Bryant, Tamera (2005). The Life & Times of Hammurabi. Bear: Mitchell Lane Publishers.

in Hesiod's *Theogony* but has been immortalized in Euripides' tragedy by the same name) and Circe (who bewitched Ulysseus' men in Homer's *Odyssey*), witchcraft wasn't really gender specific in the Pagan world in terms of who practiced it. In fact, in Africa, in the Yoruba tradition, witchcraft-practicing men were considered more common and dignified than women (who were viewed with suspicion if they practiced it).

When it comes down to it though, most deities connected to witchcraft, from Hecate in Greece to Freya in Scandinavia, were female. And perhaps that made the difference in the eyes of Christians who were looking for scapegoats… Because women, in the Middle Ages, were a much easier target than men, socially — especially if they were unmarried or widows.

But here's the thing: witchcraft was forbidden in Europe since 900 CE, considered "a trick of the devil" (yet another attempt to stifle Pagan traditions). Most people either didn't believe witches were real, considering them a fable and superstition, or knew better and stayed silent. In many parts of Europe, where the Pagan roots were still strong, witchcraft was considered a minor offence and if someone was caught they were expected to do some penance and that was it.

For the most part, practitioners of the Craft could still do rituals in secret or operate under the radar. But Heinrich Kramer changed all that.

A monk of the Dominican Order, Kramer was obsessed with witches all his life. In one of his visits in the Tyrol region of Germany he got into an altercation with a woman called Helena Scheuberin, who didn't approve of his methods and was audacious enough to speak her mind. (The horror! Can you imagine, dear one? Speaking your mind as a woman in the Middle Ages?)

Kramer brought this woman, along with six other local women, to trial for witchcraft, citing her sexual life as one of his arguments. Thankfully the local bishop was a reasonable man and sent Kramer home telling him he was crazy.

Kramer, seething at this insult, wrote "Malleus Maleficarum" (or as it is alternatively known, "The Hammer of Witches") as an act of revenge against the bishop and all those who refused to believe that "magic is a real threat" — but also revenge against women like Scheuberin who dared to speak their minds. In this book, Kramer provided detailed instructions on how to identify witches who, according to his arguments, were mostly women.

He didn't stop at identifying them: Malleus Maleficarum also offers excessive details on how to hunt them, interrogate them and punish them.

Sounds crazy, right? Something today we'd view basically as hate speech... But Kramer took his book to the Pope, the Pope liked it and gave it his seal of approval... The book became so popular, it was a bestseller in Europe — surpassed only by the Bible. And as a result, more than 80,000 women were burned at the stake or otherwise tortured to death between 1500-1660 CE under charges of "witchcraft". Who were these women? Were they witches?

Some of them, perhaps. But most of them were just unfortunate enough to have been born at a time and place where just being a woman, especially unmarried or a widow, was enough to draw suspicion on you (especially beautiful women who were thought to reject the sexual advances of powerful men). And if this horror wasn't enough, innocent animals were also burned with them. Mostly cats, who also had the misfortune of being associated with the Devil — probably due to the fact that Freya, the Scandinavian goddess of beauty who was also a witch, rode a chariot carried by flying cats... If you're feeling sick to your stomach, it's only normal. Those were horrendous times indeed. But do you see know, dear one, how far we've come? Do you see why being able to joke about being a witch on Instagram is disrespectful to all those women who died for the mere suspicion of being one?

I hope you see that. I hope you see how lucky you are to be able to make this choice and live your magickal life out in the open.

So where does that leave the Pagan world of old?

Well, depends on where in the world you look — and how eurocentric you are (as many of us, unfortunately, still tend to be).

Pagan traditions in Africa had been flourishing since time immemorial; each tribe (and later on, country) of this vast continent having their own beliefs, passed down from generation to generation through word of mouth. Many of these beliefs and pantheons, like the Yoruba religion of Nigeria and the Vodun religion of Benin, Togo and Ghana, came with them to the Americas around 1500 CE when the colonization and slave trade destroyed so many lives... Although in slavery though, these people found strength in their Pagan beliefs (very often also practiced in secret as their masters wanted them to convert to Christianity) and in time these traditions were embedded with local beliefs. Vodun in particular, became the base for practices that are alive and well to this day in Haiti, Cuba, Brazil, Puerto Rico and Louisiana.

A whole book dedicated to the Yoruba and Vodun and their branches wouldn't be enough to do justice to these rich, Pagan traditions... But we'll try to cover some of their symbols and beliefs in the third part of the book, dear one. For now it's enough to say that the colonizers may have enslaved so many people from the African continent but they failed to enslave their minds and spirits... and the colonizers' descendants are now buying magic potions and tarot sessions from their descendants on Instagram. Ain't life a funny thing? Balance always gets restored, although it may take a few generations.

But let's get back to Europe, for a moment. As the Middle Ages gave way to the Renaissance, Paganism started winning ground again — as did a strong revival of magic. How did that happen? Weren't witches supposedly all burned at the stake? Well, now. Have you forgotten that the true practitioners of witchcraft were always women AND men? The rituals and the traditions stayed alive, only they became more theoretical and esoteric, out of fear of retribution. Soon, during the era of Romanticism (from 1780 CE to 1850 CE), artists and writers found themselves drawn back to Nature, as well as to the aesthetics and folklore of Pagan medieval times and an idolized version of Ancient Greece and its pantheon.

Witchcraft and magic, Vikings and their Norse gods and goddesses, became a source of wonder. Although, of course, given the times, it was mostly wealthy white men who dabbled with magic or expressed that wonder — as the repercussions for them were close to nonexistent...

LET'S TALK ABOUT SALEM, SHALL WE?

Which brings us to the hot topic of Salem, Massachusetts.

In 1692, witch hunting had subsided in Europe — but the freshly colonized New World (only 80 or so years had gone by since the first American colony was founded in Virginia) was still a bit slow in adapting trends. So when two young girls were (as it is now believed) poisoned by a hallucination inducing fungus, mass hysteria quickly ensued believing witches were responsible for cursing them... leading to the Salem witch trials.

During the Salem witch trials, 200 people were tortured and coerced to confession of using witchcraft to harm people. One of them, Tituba, an enslaved woman, confessed that she was a witch (all the rest maintained their innocence, until their tragic deaths). 19 people were burned at the stake, 5 of which men. Witch burning took over in a few other states as well, before thankfully dying out. Ironically enough, it is today acknowledged amid the magical community that there were no real, practicing witches in Salem back in the day... but many of them have moved to that area since some theatrical plays and TV shows of the middle of last century started showing a more appealing face to magic and gave Salem its moniker as "Witch City".

Nowadays, those women and men who burned at the stake in the Salem Witch Trials are considered martyrs in the local magickal community. If anything, magick is celebrated in Salem (although through a glamorized lens, associated with overspending in witch memorabilia).

One cannot help but wonder how Kramer would feel about that...

Hopefully his spirit has moved on and learned better than to torture women by now.

Chapter 3: Paganism Today

We're almost at the end of our historical journey. We've seen the rise and fall of Pagan civilizations, we've seen the prosecutions and the mandatory conversions to Christianity; we've also seen the tide beginning to change and Paganism becoming cool again.

In a way, we are now at the most important part of our journey of understanding.

In this chapter, we're going to talk about how the 19th and the 20th century gave us so many of the tools, rituals and frame of reference we're using today as modern Pagans, Wiccans and Witches. We're going to talk about how things like spirit consultations and tarot cards came to be and how the secret societies shaped ceremonial magick. Yes, magick with a k.

You'll see, in a while.

Are you ready, dear one?

PAINTINGS, REVOLUTIONS, OCCULT SOCIETIES

Remember how we talked about the age of Romanticism earlier, where white men (mostly artists at first) started expressing an interest in all things occult? Perhaps reading this book so far will have helped you realize this: behind most trends associated with Paganism, either pro or against it, the motives are usually political.

This case is not that much different.

During the 19th century, the Western world changed a lot. Several revolutions, starting with the French in 1789 and then the Greeks who revolted against the Turks after a 400-year occupation and succeeded to gain their independence, changed the face of Europe. Around 1848, revolutions across Germany, Austria, Hungary, Italy, Denmark and Poland created new national, independent states from the ashes of old kingdoms and empires. There was a feeling of returning to one's roots and traditions, of defining what makes a nation unique and separate from its neighbors. It may not come as a surprise that this return to folk traditions in order to foster a feeling of national identity and pride, awoke many Paganism practices as well!

It happen more organically than you'd expect. For instance, writers started realizing the tremendous wealth of their national mythologies and started compiling and retelling fairy tales and myths of old (is there anything more Pagan than that?). It was during that time for instance that the Brothers Grimm wrote their (originally much more grizzly than the watered down versions we are familiar with today) fairy tales and Elias Lönnrot compiled Finnish mythology into an epic poetry work, *Kalevala*[12].

Paintings and music soon followed. Before you know it, witches and ancient goddesses, rituals and mythical creatures were depicted in paintings of prestigious painters, lauded in poems and theater plays following in the Shakespearean tradition. [It needs to be said: William Shakespear was a Pagan admirer way before it was cool, during the most difficult century for Paganism between 1500-1600 CE. He included Greek mythological characters, Pagan gods and goddesses and the practice of witchcraft in many of his works. Astonishingly enough, his sorcerers weren't always female, or always evil. Hmm, could he be onto something?]

This fascination with Pagan practices may have started with fairytales and art, but it didn't stay in that theoretical realm for

---

[12] Friberg, Eino; Landström, Björn; Schoolfield, George C., eds. (1988), The Kalevala: Epic of the Finnish People.

long. The 19th and 20th century also herald the beginning of many secret societies and sects that either practiced witchcraft in some form or theorized about it.

The Hermetic Order of the Golden Dawn

The most interesting secret society of the time was probably The Hermetic Order of the Golden Dawn or simply, Golden Dawn. At some point they were so famous in Victorian England, they weren't that much of a secret at all. They even made the news often.

To understand them a bit better, we first need to talk about Hermetic traditions in general. Yes, this is going to be another trip through time — but rest assured it will be a brief one.

After the death of Alexander the Great (who managed to conquer most of the then-known world within his short life, before dying at 33 years old in 323 BCE), the Kingdoms of Babylon, Egypt and the Near East in general were never the same. Certainly, the people who lived there were still mostly locals, but since their rulers, the heirs of Alexander, were of Greek descent, every aspect of life, culture and religion was glimpsed through a Hellenistic lens. Since the Egyptian Pantheon had many similarities to the Greek one, that last thing wasn't so hard to do either.

That's when Hermes Trismegistus ("thrice great") started being worshipped. Hermes Trismegistus was basically an amalgamation of Hermes (the Greek god of communication, or Mercury as it became his Latin name) and Thoth, the Egyptian god of wisdom. Old Thoth temples were now used to worship this "new and improved" version of the god and quickly his worship became a big thing during that time period.

How does that affect the 19th century Europe, you ask?

Well, the texts written based on that worship, the Hermetic texts, were basically instructions on how to perform witchcraft in a sophisticated and philosophical manner[13]. Created (mostly) by men, for (mostly) men. They combined astrology practices that were very popular with the Babylonias of the time, with alchemy (the practice of turning a substance, say coal, to another substance, say gold) and animistic practices (like spirit conjuring and animating statues, yes, really, it was based on the belief that everything has a soul). Most importantly, these Hermetic texts were written in a way that cauterized systemic religion and geared towards personal development; towards making one's self ascend to something greater, an existence that goes beyond the physical.

These Hermetic texts maintained a prominence throughout the ages. Some Christian scholars saw Hermes Trismegistus as a foreteller of Christian God; the early Muslims believed he built the

---

[13] Yates, Frances A., Giordano Bruno and the Hermetic Tradition. University of Chicago Press, 1964.

pyramids of Giza – he's even mentioned (not by name, but implied) in the Quran. So although of course these texts were considered Pagan of origin, they were not condemned like other Pagan texts were during the Middle Ages. On the contrary, the Hermetic texts gained great notoriety in Europe, especially because of their dialectic on how to control Nature (which was a big thing back then). They helped a new generation of people who combined science and a quest for knowledge with occult wisdom, like Italian philosopher and wizard Giordano Bruno, emerge. In fact, even Sir Isaan Newton studied these Hermetic texts to help him "understand the world better." Yes, the guy who brought us the law of gravity was also a low-key wizard.

But then again, everyone who was someone was a low-key wizard back then. Which brings us full-circle to the creation of Golden Dawn[14].

In a way, Golden Dawn was an evolution of Freemasonry: its three founders were all Freemasons and the organization followed the tenets of Freemasonry in terms of creating different grades of hierarchy and initiation; different "Orders". But whereas in Freemasonry the focus is mostly on creating bonds of fraternity and

---

[14] Runyon, Carroll (1997). Secrets of the Golden Dawn Cipher Manuscripts. C.H.S.

helping each other in distress (providing along the way "secrets" that can benefit and improve the lives of its members), in Golden Dawn the focus was in studying the Hermetic texts and practicing ceremonial witchcraft and metaphysics experiments. Plus, unlike in Freemasonry, women were allowed in Golden Dawn. Perhaps because of that, around 1895 CE the secret organization was so well established in Victorian England that had more than 100 members, many contemporary celebrities and artists (like the poet Yeats) among them.

One of these celebrities of the time was Aleister Crowly.

The part where Aleister Croley deserves a book of his own

Crowley was many things: a poet, a painter, an author, a world traveler; a mountaineer and (according to some sources) a spy for the British Intelligence. He's influenced Yeats; written poems for the painter Rodin, whom he knew; wrote articles for Vanity Fair and prominent astrology columns of the time; performed sex magick with movie stars; got deported from two countries; impregnated several women most of whom not married to him; had many male lovers; faked his death with the help of Portuguese writer Fernando Pessoa... Crowley was, originally, "fascinated" by Adolf Hitler — at least until he realized the extent of the threat of nazism and condemned Hitler and his practices by calling him "a black magician".

Yeah. It does make you wonder how Hollywood hasn't turned his life into a movie yet. (Although the name Crowley has been used in several TV shows to describe fictional demons.)

He's also the reason we write magick with a k: he started writing the word like that based on its more archaic spelling, to differentiate it from the common parlor tricks of stage magicians and illusionists (like Houdini) who were also starting to become popular during that time.

Aleister Crowley joined the secret society of Golden Dawn in 1898 and progressed until the Second Order, at the grade of Adeptus Minor. His mere ascendance to that final grade caused such conflict within the Golden Dawn ranks, the society's founder was practically kicked out for helping him ascend. Why? Well, Crowley was a divisive figure — he enjoyed being one.

It wasn't just his open bi-sexuality, promiscuity and drug abuse that made him polarizing in the eyes of his Victorian contemporaries. It was mostly the fact that he believed he was a prophet of an ancient Egyptian being, destined to guide humanity into the "Æon of Horus". The Aeon of Horus, in contrast to the Aeon of Osiris which Crowley thought humanity was currently experiencing (where patriarchy and monotheism ruled) or the older Aeon of isis (where

Crowley saw as that time in humanity where matriarchal values and the worship of the goddess were more prominent) was supposed to usher in a new era for mankind. An era of ascendance and self-realization — a philosophy that was very close to the core message of the Hermetic texts.

Even more polarizing, was how he got this idea.

Apparently, after spending some time in Scotland and traveling to Mexico and India, where he studied Buddhism and Hinduism, Crowley and his then wife honeymooned in Egypt, where they visited the pyramids. (Remember how we elaborated on the power of the pyramids on the previous chapter and how they were built to connect the sun with the underworld and act as chambers of resurrection?)

Apparently they had some kind of profound experience there, because soon after they turned their rented apartment in Cairo into a temple where they invoked Egyptian deities. His wife, Rose, started getting messages from spirits and informed Crowley that there were beings who waited to communicate with him. A few weeks after that, Crowley himself was contacted by a being he called Aiwass, who apparently dictated him a book, from beginning to end, which Crowley finished writing in three days.

The Book of the Law became the basis for Thelema, the religion Crowley later on founded. The premise of Thelema is "Do what thou wilt shall be the whole of the Law[15]," urging people to live only according to their own True Will and use magick as a tool for self-actualization. Crowley's book and religion became a tremendous influence both to his contemporaries and to the students of magick, the occult arts and self-actualization that came after. It is rumored that the founder of Scientology, L. Ron Hubbard, was deeply inspired by Crowley and involved in Thelema. It is also widely acknowledged that Crowly and Thelema inspired Gerald Gardner to found Wicca... but more on that in the next part of the book!

Apart from Golden Dawn, which the disagreement about him caused a schism in some of its temples, Crowley founded and participated in other esoteric orders, like the A∴A∴ and the German-based O.T.O. (Ordo Templi Orientis), through which he preached and propagated Thelema. The religion was spread to the US and Australia besides Europe and by 1920 Crowley had established an Abbey in Sicily where he lived in communion with his followers and participated in various rituals that very often included sadomasochistic versions of sex magick, influenced by his studies in Tantra yoga. He also created his own tarot deck, the Thoth tarot deck, where the Major Arcana cards follow a different

---

[15] Crowley, Aleister. The Equinox of the Gods. New Falcon Publications, 1991.

order — he felt that the popular Rider-Waite tarot deck was more intended for laymen and less for actual occult students.

(We'll cover more of this on the third part of the book where we'll discuss the Tarot.)

The press of the time didn't see eye to eye with him. One newspaper in particular, loved to publish defamatory stories about him — they called him a Satanist, an advocate of human sacrifice and "the wickedest man in the world". Although he often thought about suing that paper, Crowley's lifestyle and his lifelong struggle with his heroin addiction always left him strapped for cash. He ended up having to accept bizarre work offers (from advisor to rich people to astrology column writer) and welcomed notoriety as a means to keep spreading the word of Thelema.

In his "autohagiography" (like an autobiography, but for self-proclaimed saints and we're saying this with as little irony as possible) Crowley explained that his ultimate vision was one of restoring Paganism to a purer form. After his extensive studies in various Asian occult traditions and religious philosophies, he wanted to combine "oriental wisdom" with the Hermetic philosophy and ceremonial magick of the Hermetic traditions.

Regardless of how one feels about Aleister Crowley and his approach to witchcraft, his charisma and influence cannon be debated. His legacy to this day is that of a man who awoke the thirst for occult knowledge in the 20th century; someone who inspired people to study and try to understand magick.

Magick with a k, of course.

Honoring the Past, Redefining the Present

After Alister Crowley's Thelema rose in popularity, modern Paganism really caught on — first in Europe and then in the US, Australia and South Africa. Also called "neo-Paganism", this new wave of honoring and following the old Pagan traditions quickly became as diverse as its practitioners. It turns out, dear one, that it's the most Pagan thing to do.

So what does it mean to be a Pagan in this day and age — that may be the Aeon of Horus or just the Aeon of Instagram?

It really depends on how you see yourself in relation to your ancestors. For instance, many modern practitioners or Paganism and Witchcraft are indeed direct descendants of the Yoruba and Vodun practitioners of old, who came to the Americas when they were brought into slavery by the colonizers. But the ancestry line of European Paganism is not as easy to identify — and this is an important subject that we'll cover in the next part of the book, when we talk about Wicca and Witchcraft.

What it boils down to is that some Modern Pagans are trying to revive the old religions (picking a single religion that believe is closer to their heritage or personality) as faithfully as they can, by even dressing the part, whereas others prefer to borrow different elements from many different Pagan practices of old and create their unique blend of Paganism. The first are called reconstructionists, the second are called eclectic.

Wicca, which we'll go into detail later, is an example of a new Pagan religion with eclectic elements, as it combines shamanic practices of Native Americans with Celtic Druidry and Thelema ceremonies. There are also the practitioners of Crowley's Thelema to this day, those who practice modern Druidism or Hellenism, those who practice Odinism (Norse Paganism) or Heathenry (Germanic Paganism with a contemporary twist), those who practice Stregheria (an Italian version of Wicca, focusing on local medieval traditions of witchcraft).

Some modern Pagans will also combine elements from monotheistic religions such as Buddhism, Judaism and Christianity, not feeling that one clashes with the other. I personally know many fellow Pagans who believe in Angels (Archangel Michael in particular) and pray to both Madonna, the Holy Mother of Jesus (who many historians argue that her sanctification and worship was a way to entice Pagans who were used to worshiping Goddesses), wear the

Cross and have Pagan altars dedicated to gods and goddesses… Does that sound weird to you?

If it hasn't been clear in this book so far, we don't believe one way of going about it is inherently better than the other. You'll need to forge your own Path and decide what's included in it.

We'll talk about it more in our next chapter.

Chapter 4: How Do You Know You're a Pagan

How do you, indeed?

If that long, 2-chapter history lesson taught us anything, dear one, apart from the fact that burning people at the stake is as bad as throwing them to the lions, is that there is no set or "authentic" way to be Pagan.

Being Pagan is being in touch with Nature — and the only constant of Nature is change. As the Wheel turns, so do our beliefs, our habits and our priorities. With new seasons comes new understanding. What you consider the core of your Pagan identity today there's a big chance it won't be the core of your Pagan identity a few years from now or further down the line.

Trust on this to happen.

So… what? Abandon all attempts at a definition? Of course not!

History, at least the abridged version of it we attempted to embark earlier, has taught us that a Pagan is someone who perseveres; who adapts. The person who speaks their mind even if they know the situation may not be in their favor (like Helena Scheuberin who stood up to Kramer). The person who knows that rational thought and scientific research is all well and good, but it's not all there is. The person who is not afraid to go against the grain, think outside the box or even make the box disappear altogether! The person who most of all, understands that Nature is a manifestation of our Divine Mother and for that deserves our utmost respect and protection.

(Is Greta Thunberg a Pagan, you ask? I don't believe so, dear one. But she does share and preach some very fundamental Pagan values and for that, we salute her.)

But seriously, no Pagan would ever do anything to hurt Nature for no reason: sure, Pagans used to cut down trees to chop wood for fire or to build their houses, but they were always careful not to chop too many trees in one area, because they knew the consequences once the first heavy rainfall fell. Pagans liked profit as much as the next man, but they knew that if they overextended themselves or completely depleted their resources they would be the ones to suffer. So many modern humans seem to have forgotten this — it's mind blowing, really!

A Pagan understands balance. A Pagan understands there are things bigger than our egos or our wallets or our rational explanations for things. A Pagan will never be dismissive of the dark when out in the woods, because although they know they're probably perfectly safe, they still feel a sense of awe for all the energies out there. They do not wish to disturb the night if they don't have to. They don't need to prove their superiority to Nature. They know better.

We've been talking a lot about Nature, it's true.

Can't you be a true Pagan and live in a city?

Of course, dear one! What did we say about no set or "authentic" way of being a Pagan?

Many Pagans nowadays still choose to live in the big cities. They thrive from the hustle and bustle, the energies of the different people they meet, the openness of diverse cultures and the many opportunities to celebrate. Yes, a Pagan likes to celebrate when it's time to celebrate.

That's not to say that to identify as a Pagan you have to be a party animal who'd make even the Romans blush. But all Pagans understand that our bodies come from Nature and we have to respect them, to give them their due. And that is true both when it comes to our sexuality and to our relationship with food.

Would a Pagan ever go on a diet, you ask? Probably not, at least not to adhere to some society's beauty standards. But they would most definitely change their eating habits in order to feel better/stronger/lighter or whatever better health looks like to them. Plus, all Pagans respect food too much to ever associate it with guilt. Even if they consume animal products (which many of us choose to abstain from) they do so consciously and with respect to the life forces that have been sacrificed for their nourishment. Some Pagans even prefer to hunt their own game.

Guilt, as mentioned earlier, is another key word here. Guilt has been the driving force behind many monotheistic religions: guilt, fear and promises of a better life after death if we're being pious enough in this one. Of course Pagans will experience some guilt throughout their lives (we are human, after all). But their guilt will come from their own actions or lack thereof: from things they did or didn't do, mostly to other people. This is a different guilt than the guilt inflicted on people by society or religion, for all the things they are not allowed to do in order to be "good".

To get back to the sexuality part, not all Pagans are as promiscuous and hedonistic as medieval gravures would paint us to be. Some are still experimenting; some are in long, committed relationships; some have chosen a solitary path or prefer platonic relationships. But whatever they do, they understand that sex is a part of life. Sacred, sometimes. Mundane, other times. A taboo, never. This kind of morality, of denying one's urges to appear pious in front of a god or a society that would judge them, is just not interesting to a Pagan. We make our own moral code, based on what feels right to each of us.

Are Pagans bad? Well, some of them are, dear one. Being a Pagan does not exempt you from certain aspects of humanity and not everyone you'll meet out there has your best interests at heart. Trust this to be true as well. But the point of this chapter is for you to understand that all kinds of people can be Pagan. The question then becomes: what kind of person are you?

And what kind of Pagan will you be?

Hopefully, you'll be someone who listens to their heard, always. Someone who sees the wonder in the everyday and makes no excuses for their path and their choices. Someone who knows there are things out there we will never be able to explain but also someone who will never stop being intrigued by the unknown; the hidden; the occult. Someone who honors their ancestors; those who came before us, whose sacrifice and wisdom has paved the way for our existence.

Someone who may or may not combine elements from different Pagan paths to craft their own. Someone who may or may not practice magic, but who definitely knows magic is all around us. To paraphrase the song, "I feel it in my fingers, I feel it in my toes."

Yes, that song is about Christmas. But we already established Christmas were more or less invented by Pagans, didn't we? So it's kinda ours to steal.

PART 2: WICCA

CHAPTER 1: WICCA THEN AND NOW

Welcome back, dear one. It has been quite a ride, reading about Paganism, hasn't it?

Now that you understand what it means to be a Pagan (and hopefully have started thinking about the kind of Pagan you'd like to be), it's time to discuss Wicca. Wiccan is part of Modern Paganism; it's one Path you can take out of many. The reason why we've chosen to focus on Wicca more than on other forms of Modern Paganism in this book, is because Wicca is the largest Modern Pagan religion (followed by Neo-Druidism). It's a diverse Path that has changed and enriched so many people's lives all over the world…

Perhaps, dear one, it will also change yours.

But first things first: what exactly is Wicca and how it came to be? This is what we'll attempt to answer in this chapter.

GERALD GARDNER AND THE GHOST OF ALEISTER CROWLEY

We briefly mentioned, in the first part of the book, about the effect Aleister Crowley had in the occult community of the late 19th and early 20th century — to the point that he and his religion, Thelema, served as a major inspiration for the founder of Wicca, Gerald Gardner.

(I do hope you haven't skipped that part of the book, there's important information there that will help you understand the rest of the book... You haven't? That's the spirit, keep reading!)

Who was Gerald Gardner then?

Frequently called the "Father of Wicca", Gardner's interest in the occult can be traced in the years he spent as a civil servant for the UK in Singapore, where he became fascinated by the magickal practices and traditions of the locals. After retirement and a brief respite in Cyprus where he wrote a novel, Garner returned to England where he lived near the New Forest, a historical woods in

Southern England that's been proclaimed a royal forest since 1079 CE. There was a significant occult community in the area and Gardner eventually joined an occult organization called the Rosicrucian Order Crotona Fellowship.

The Rosicrucians, a bit similar to the Golden Dawn, was an esoteric organization seeking "knowledge that is hidden to many". One of the differences with Golden Dawn however, is that their practices apart from Hermetism, Kabbalah and alchemy also include mystical Christianity.

Gardner wasn't particularly impressed with the Fellowship, especially with their Grand Master's claims of being Pythagoras reincarnate (among other things). When one of the Fellowship's leaders in 1939 sent a letter to every member claiming that war would not reach Britain and the very next day the Crown declared war on Germany, Gardner was practically convinced there was no real power or wisdom within that organization.

Through this organization though, Gardner made an acquaintance that changed his whole life.

The Father of Wicca recounts[16] him and the Fellowship visiting the house of a local woman one night, where he went through a

---

[16] Gerald Gardner, (1954). Witchcraft Today. London: Rider.

ceremony of initiation skyclad (naked). There, he heard the word "Wica" — which he recognized as an old form of the word "witch". Back then, there was a historical theory made prominent by archaeologist Margaret Murray: that the persecution of witches in the 1500-1600 CE was an organized attempt to erase from history a pagan religion devoted to a Horned God[17]. (Which wasn't entirely wrong, but it made the mistake of painting all the different Pagan traditions and beliefs with the same brush, as well as assuming the women who were burned at the stake were actually witches and not mostly victims of patriarchal and social violence.) In any case, when Gardner heard the word "Wica", he was convinced that Murray's claims were true and that the coven he'd visited was a continuation of that ancient Pagan religion that had survived the brutal witch burnings of the Middle Ages...

He became fascinated with this group. Despite him always being very open to the press (to the point that he has been accused by his contemporaries of being a publicity w**re), he never revealed the ceremonies he witnessed with that coven — apart from one ceremony that was meant to ward off the Nazi invasion to England.

---

[17] Murray, Margaret A. (1921). The Witch-Cult in Western Europe. Oxford: Clarendon Press and Murray, Margaret A. (1931). The God of the Witches. London: Faber and Faber.

The witches, according to Gardner, formed a circle in the woods one night to raise a "cone of power" to send to Berlin…

Could it be that it was witches who helped the allies win WWII? There is no way to know, dear one. Certainly, stranger things have happened throughout the course of history.

But let's get back to Gerald Gardner.

His eclectic interest in different occult practices, specifically esoteric Christianity, led him to become an ordained priest of the Ancient British Church. He also joined ADO (the Ancient Druid Order) with whom he attended rituals at Stonehenge. (Remember the importance of Stonehenge and the way it was built? Its draw to Pagans still remains strong to this day…) Gardner didn't stop there: he joined the Folk-Lore Society, the Society for Psychical Research and, ultimately, the O.T.O., after meeting Aleister Crowley.

Gardner's fascination with Crowley has been the subject of many biographies and historical research… A fascination that seems mutual, considering that Crowley, right before he died, issued a charter decreeing that Gardner was to undertake one of the most important positions in O.T.O. after his death. By that time, Gardner had already started creating his version of Wicca rituals based on his observations of the New Forest coven — and as these rituals worshipped the Divine Female alongside the Horned God, he had initiated many High Priestesses to the Craft. Crowley, according to Gardner, was thinking about joining Wicca but he disliked the idea of "being bossed about by women". According to other sources, however, he was initiated in Wicca in secret and has in fact written many of the rituals that are attributed to Gardner himself.

It's a bit of a headache at this point, isn't it, dear one?

What we need to take away from all this is that the need to find kindred spirits has been ever present throughout humanity's history. Isn't that one of the reasons you picked up this book?

These two, clearly powerful and emblematic men, were looking for answers all their lives and did no small amount of experimenting to find them. They both envisioned a more self-actualized humanity, and they both felt the need to "dress up" their practices and rituals with something bigger than themselves: in Crowley's case the Egyptian god that was revealed to him in the pyramids, in Gardner's case, the uncovering of a secret cult that had survived for centuries... Regardless of whether their claims were 100% truthful or not (as historians remain sceptical on both counts), these two men practically created a Modern Pagan revival that helped thousands of people to find their place in the world; people who felt alienated by Christianity and monotheism.

Of course, like most emblematic figures, both men were very polarizing. They both joined secret organizations (in Crowley's case, Golden Dawn, in Gardner's case the Rosicrucians) where he caused a stir with the rest of the members and ultimately struck out on their own. Gardner may not have been called "the world's most wicked man" by the press (although there were some headlines that he was preaching "devil worship"), but he was called a "hack" and a "fraud" by many, due to his tendency to overextend the truth — especially when it came to his formal qualifications, where he always claimed he had more degrees than he actually had.

After Crowley's death, Gardner believed he would be his successor in O.T.O but when that didn't happen he decided to focus on the witch-cult he (believed he) unearthed in New Forest. He was adamant in his mission to revive the Old Religion and awakening people's interest in witchcraft and wrote many books about it (including detailed rituals that usually involved ceremonial nudity, scourging and incantations) that gathered a lot of attention. His most popular book, Witchcraft Today, was prefaced by Margaret Murray who basically endorsed him and supported his claim about the coven being the descendants of those witches who didn't die in the Middle Ages.

Gardner formed his own coven in London, where he initiated many people into the Craft, many of which moved on to spread the word of Wicca in the US and Australia in the following decades. Sadly, he had a falling out with many of his former friends and priests/priestesses of Wicca, who left what is now called "Gardnerian Wicca" to start their own Wicca traditions.

THE GARDNERIAN LEGACY AND THE MANY BRANCHES OF WICCA

Since we talked about the "Father of Witchcraft", it would be only fair to talk about the "Mother of Modern Witchcraft" next, right? Her name was Doreen Valiente.

Valiente met Gardner in 1952 (when she started corresponding with him after having read articles about him and Wicca) and was initiated into the craft in 1953. She rose quickly through the ranks and became his coven's High Priestess — to the point where she revised Gardner's Book of Shadows, removing Aleister Crowley's influence (most of it, at least) and added an emphasis to Divine Femininity with Goddess prayers[18].

Valiente ultimately grew weary of Gardner's love for press and attention and left Gardnerian Wicca along with her followers. She

---

[18] Valiente, Doreen (1989). The Rebirth of Witchcraft. London: Robert Hale.

experimented with different Wicca branches that had started to emerge by then (more of that in a while), joined the Pagan Front and the Witchcraft Research Association and wrote various magazine articles and books promoting Wicca. A big departure of Valiente from the Gardnerian tradition is that she believed anyone could be a Wiccan, no "skyclad" initiation by a Wiccan High Priest or Priestess needed.

In a way, dear one, the fact that you're able to read this book and learn some Wicca rituals, we both owe to Daphne Valiente. And for that, we give thanks to the Mother of Modern Witchcraft.

One of the Wicca branches Valiente worked with briefly was Charles Cardell's.

Starting as Gardner's friend and coven member, Cardell had a huge falling out with him — to the point where he wrote many defamatory articles about Gardner. In those articles, among other things, Cardell claimed he was the one to first use the term "Wicca" and to this day his followers are called "Wiccens". His version of Wicca included worshipping a Horned God called Atho and in his publications he antagonized both Gardner and Valiente. Yes, he fell out with her as well. (Valiente actually was disappointed by Cardell being dishonest, when he tried to convince her that some contemporary items he possessed were magical relics from Pompei…) But it was Cardell's way of falling out with everyone, it seems: he also fell out with another Wiccan friend, Raymond Howard, who even took Cardell to court accusing him of hexing him.

Doesn't that sound awfully like the two men from the Code of Hammurabi, casting hexes at each other? It's fascinating to see that, for all the wisdom Magick can bring into one's heart, we are ultimately humans and our egos can always get the best of us...

Anyway, Raymon Howard himself continued the Coven of Atho — he even claimed he had a 2200 years old statue of the god (which was later revealed he'd carved himself).

Another important Wicca personality of the time was Eleanor "Ray" Bone, who is known as the "Matriarch of British Witchcraft". Bone created many covens and furthered the practice of Gardnerian Wicca (also believing that the New Forest coven was the continuation of an ancient tradition) evolving it into what is now also called British Traditional Wicca. Bone had a fall out (as it seems to have been the early Wicca fashion) with Alex Sanders, who went on to create his own version of Wicca called "Alexandrian" that includes more elements of ceremonial magic and Qabalah. Alexandrian Wicca is more technical, with more rigorous training and ceremonial practices, but also more eclectic and less hesitant in borrowing techniques from other traditions. In fact, their motto is "if it works, use it". Contrary to Valiente's tradition though, in

Alexandrian Wicca you have to be initiated by another witch — it's not an open club.

Let's take a breath, dear one, shall we?

So many names, and so many of them fighting one another! You may have started feeling that Wicca is not very inviting — and that's definitely not the case. You have to consider that back then, in the 60s and 70s, rediscovering the Pagan ways felt (and was) revolutionary. Everyone wanted to make their own mark into this new movement. In the end, that's a good thing.

It's through all these different, often conflicting, viewpoints, Wicca became what it is today: a vibrant religion with many different branches, where there is something for everyone…

In the United States, the Gardnerian and Alexandrian Wicca traditions were combined into what became Blue Star Wicca, that still emphasizes initiation but also accepts solitary practitioners and people who are both polytheists and monotheists. Blue Star Wiccans are all about giving back to the community and including a lot of music and singing in their rituals — they also have initiatory tattoos. Blue Star Wicca is still practiced as a Wicca branch in the US.

In Canada, the Odyssean Wicca is most prominent (they chose the name to imply the "spiritual journey" one must go through).

Odysseans follow the British Traditional Wicca but in a more eclectic way. They have a public Wiccan priesthood and a very rigorous training system (like in the Alexandrian tradition), not accepting new students easily.

Another notable Wicca branch is Zsuzsanna Budapest's Dianic Wicca, also in the States. Dianic Wicca is the only version of Wicca that's female-only: they only worship the Goddess (in contrast to the duality of a Goddess and a God in most Wiccan traditions) and do not accept men in their covens. They've also borrowed many elements from the folk magick traditions of Italy as well as various healing practices from many cultures. It may sound weird and a bit sexist perhaps, but Dianic Wicca is first and foremost a welcoming place for women who have been victims of violence or abuse and are looking for a way to reconnect with their inner power...

Told you there' something for everyone in Wicca, dear one.

Wicca today

After reading through all that you may be wondering: what, exactly, is Wicca today?

What do these Wiccans believe in?

The answer to that may be slightly different depending on who you ask (and what tradition they follow). Wiccans, like all Pagans, have an inherent dislike of homogeneity. Each Wicca branch prefers marching to the beat of their own drum (sometimes literally) and although Wicca is recognized as a religion, there is no central authority figure like a Pope or an Orthodox Patriarch. Although Gardner's and Valiente's texts are widely spread, along with the texts of other writers such as Starhawk or the earlier works of Charles Godfrey Leland (his book *Aradia, the Gospel of Witches* was actually the seed for Margaret Murray's and Gardner's theory of an existing ancient coven), many Wiccans will also study sacred texts from other religions, like the Bible or the Torah, or even create their own, eclectic mix of traditions.

But for all their distinct personalities, there are some broad lines all Wiccans adhere to.

First of all, Wicca is an Earth-based religion — which means there is an inherent respect of Nature and a belief in a cyclical view of the time (the Wheel of the Year). Apart from Dianic Wicca, all other traditions believe in the duality of a Goddess and a God, who are basically the yin and yang expressions of all energies in the Universe: some people perceive these gods as abstractions or even Jungian archetypes, whereas others consider them as real as a devout Christian considers God. The gods of Wicca have a loving relationship between them and evolve with the seasons. The male forms of god in Wicca change on a yearly basis, celebrating virility and strength in Spring with the Horned God (or similar deities) and fatherly love, protection of the family and wisdom with the Oak King (or similar deities) in the Winter. The triple nature of the Goddess as Maiden, Mother and Crone is also celebrated monthly and associated with the Waxing, Full and Waning phases of the Moon.

As Wiccans nowadays come from so many different ethnic backgrounds, local deities are incorporated in people's beliefs as manifestations of the Great Goddess/Female Energy or the Great God/Male Energy. However, Wiccans are also encouraged (and the author of this book finds this very important) to educate themselves on other cultures' pantheons and decide if they feel any connection to the deities of these pantheons — and include them in their worship if they do. So for instance you can be a Wiccan who lives in Australia but worships Odin (from the Norse pantheon) and Artemis (from the Greek pantheon). Or you can be a Wiccan who lives in Greece and worship Hekate (the ancient Greek Goddess of

Witchcraft) because it's part of your heritage, but also worship Kali (from the Hindu pantheon) and Mawu (the creator goddess from the Yoruba pantheon) because they're badass ladies and you feel a connection to them.

Wiccans don't believe any god or goddess will mind sharing your affections, dear one. Or, if you decide to only worship one God or Goddess, or not worship anyone in particular and just be in awe of Nature, that's perfectly alright too.

Regardless of what you believe or don't believe in, most Wiccans have some set celebrations that they observe throughout the Wheel of the Year. These are the four Sabbats (Samhain, Imbolc, Beltan and Lamas) that continue the celebration of ancient Pagan festivals that marked the changing of the seasons, as well as the four Esbats (Yule, Ostara, Midsummer and Mabon) that correspond with the solstices and the equinoxes. In Wicca tradition, the year actually begins after Samhain, so the first day of the new year is considered November 1st — although they will also gladly celebrate with their non-Pagan friends on January 1st.

What about heaven and life after death, you ask?

If you ask ten Wiccans about their views on afterlife, you'll probably get ten different answers. Many Wiccans believe in some version of rebirth or reincarnation, because of their belief in the cyclical nature of the universe. Others will believe in some version of elevated spirit existence (like heaven or Valhalla) after death whereas others prefer not to think about it at all. The thing everyone will agree on is that this life is not a trial or a test so that we can be granted access in some paradise when we die. Our life in this world and our physical existence matter, our body matters and we owe it to ourselves and to our gods to take care of it and live a life that's as happy and fulfilled as possible!

To that extent, there is only one sacred law among all Wiccans: "an ye harm none, do what ye will" (you can encounter this phrase in different variations, but the meaning remains the same). This phrase is basically Gardner's adaptation to Crowley's Thelema law "do what thou wilt" but the idea behind it is not new. As we've seen in the first part of the book, Confucius offered a similar advice in his texts several thousand years ago… This phrase is included in a poem called the Wiccan Rede[19], which was first circulated around the '40s with the intention to pass on the old Pagan ways and traditions. Most Wiccans consider it sacred, in the sense that they will get back and consult it every now and then. The Rede talks about the Goddess and the God, the Sabbats and Esbats, about

---

[19] "The Wiccan Rede" (Full Version) as depicted in The Celtic Connection website, https://wicca.com/celtic/wicca/rede.htm

plants that are suitable for magick and about the energies of the Moon. But its core, is the Wiccan law of non harming anyone, delivered in verse.

This Wiccan law means that it goes against Wiccan beliefs to harm any other being, both humans and animals or plants — that's why you'll see many Wiccans espousing a plant-based diet and you'll probably see zero Wiccans advocating violence of any kind. Wiccans value peace. We also never, ever, use our magick to harm or hex people.

Which brings us to another key question you may have: do Wiccans cast magick spells on a daily basis? Do they even practice witchcraft at all?

That, dear one, we'll discuss in the following chapters.

Chapter 2: What Wicca Isn't… And What It Can Be

Now that we've touched upon the history of Wicca and the way it's been practiced today all around the world, it's time to clear up some issues and misconceptions that often come up.

Wicca is not the continuation of an ancient religion

"We are the descendants of the witches you could not burn." I'm sure you've seen this motto somewhere, dear one. It's been featured in everything from t-shirts to posters people have held in various demonstrations. It's a very valid sentiment, certainly.

But in most cases at least, it's just that: a sentiment.

We're not saying there are no legacy witches and Pagans out there. People who, for generations, they've worshipped the old gods and goddesses and performed various spells and rituals that were passed on from their elders. While these people, "legacies" let's call them, certainly exist, they are not the bulk of what makes modern Paganism or Wicca.

Yet, we've already seen how Margaret Murray and Gerald Gardner believed there was a secret religion and practicing covens that had escaped the witch burnings... Where did that belief come from? For the most part, it started back in 1899 with Charles Godfrey Leland and his book *Aradia, or the Gospel of the Witches*[20].

Leland was a writer and folklorist from the States who met a woman in Tuscany. That woman, whom Leland called Maddalena, claimed to be a witch — and she gave him access to lore and texts that were allegedly the sacred texts of her coven. After eleven years or working together, this woman gave Leland a manuscript she called Vangelo (which is Italian for "gospel") that narrated the story of local Moon Goddess Aradia who was worshipped among her coven apparently since medieval times. Leland basically translated

---

[20] Leland, Charles Godfrey (1899). Aradia, or the Gospel of the Witches. David Nutt.

her manuscript in English; that's how his book came about. Although the book was more or less ignored until the mid-20th century, the post-war renewal of interest in the mystic and the occult made the Gospel of Witches one of the most prominent texts, affecting people like Murray and Gardner.

Now, there may very well have been a coven in Tuscany that Leyland came across, just as there may very well have been a coven in New Forest that Gardner came across. People have been practicing witchcraft, whether solitary or in covens since time immemorial; the witch burnings certainly derailed the movement and spread terror, but it is unlikely that they shuffled out witchcraft completely (since, as we've seen, the witch burnings were mostly targeting women). But does that make the Italian witches and the English witches practitioners of the same "Old Religion"? Not really.

As we've seen, ancient Pagans always considered themselves different from their Pagan neighbors. There was never one "Pagan religion" or one way of practicing witchcraft. So what Leyland and Gardner came across, is proof that witches exist — but that's about it. Any attempts to create a common narrative, an unbroken line that goes back to the Middle Ages, were probably wishful thinking and a way to increase the credibility levels of their teachings (at least in Gardner's case). It helped create Wicca back then, that's for sure.

But we know better now.

Now we can accept Wicca for what it truly is: an eclectic reconstruction of mostly Celtic Pagan traditions, with elements from ancient Greek, Hermetic and shamanic traditions, that's also open to influences from local pantheons.

Does that make us less authentic or real? Definitely not.

Think about it in Harry Potter terms, dear one: there are pureblooded wizards and witches, like the Potters, the Malfoys and the Weasleys... but there are also wizards and witches born from "Muggle" families, like Hermione Granger, who have more talent and magical skills than most purebloods, despite being first generation. (Harry Potter is fiction, but the analogy still stands.)

The fact that you don't come from a magickal family (that you know of) doesn't mean you're cut off from magick. You know why? Because no one, ever, is really cut off from magick.

Magick, witchcraft, and honoring Nature like she deserves, have been embedded in our DNA ever since we lived in those caves and created those fertility Goddess statues we talked about in the beginning of the book. Wicca is just a modern, more organized way to access and honor all that. It is a continuation of what our ancestors believed in, in the sense that we are all humans and we all share the same common thread of existence.

WICCA IS NOT ABOUT WORSHIPING THE DEVIL

We've already seen why equating Paganism with devil worship is not just wrong, but historically inaccurate as well. This is even more true in the case of Wicca.

One of the cornerstone deities/god archetypes in Wicca is the Horned God. The Horned God draws mostly from the Celtic God Cernunnos (but also from Pan) to celebrate a non-toxic version of masculinity and male energy. The Horned God is strong and fertile, helping the Goddess create new life — but he is also fair and kind, a protector to all beings.

We are taking back the depictions of horned beings that Christianity has vilified; we are reclaiming them and reassigning them the status once had: that of beings who symbolize good luck, abundance, strength and fertility.

Now, we've already seen that the devil is a Christian invention. A way to create a strong antagonist for God and convince people that being a Pagan should be avoided at all costs. Although today many

Wiccans include elements of Christianity in their beliefs, we need to make this clear: if you ever meet a Wiccan who tells you they worship the devil, rest assured they're most definitely not really Wiccans. Why? Two reasons.

First off, this idea of an "absolute evil" is mostly a human construct. It's not something you'd ever encounter in Nature. There are destructive, chaotic energies all around us, that's for sure, but they're never 100% "bad" or "evil" because Nature doesn't have morality in the human sense. More importantly, Nature is never just one thing. Every destructive energy contains within it the seed of new creation — and the phrase "it's always darkest before the dawn" is popular for a reason.

Secondly, remember how we said that Wiccans don't necessarily agree on many things when it comes to their beliefs but they all agree on one sacred law? Remember what that sacred law is?

"An ye harm none, do what ye will."

Exactly. Wiccans believe in never hurting another being — that's why we also never make sacrifices that include shedding a creature's blood, like many ancient Pagans did and some modern Pagans do to this day. So it stands to reason that someone who abhors hurting others would definitely not worship a deity (made up by Christianity or not) that is all about being evil and hurting others.

Doesn't that make sense, dear one?

Wicca is not "witchcraft lite"

This is perhaps the most weird misconception of them all.

There is this belief, circulating in some circles, that Wicca is a "watered down" version of witchcraft, a "white-washed" way of practicing the Craft. This belief is often found among Pagan (non-Wiccan, of course) circles but also among people whose only interaction with witchcraft is what they've seen in shows and movies.

So where does this belief come from?

It starts with the name "Wicca", dear one.

See, back in the 50s when Gerald Gardner first started spreading the word, the name he used to describe this new version of the Old Religion was mostly "witch-cult", "witchcraft" or "Craft of the Wise" (or just Craft). Some times, he would circle back to the word Wica (with one c) that he heard during that New Forest coven ceremony. In fact, remember how one of his followers-cum-rivals, Charles Cardell was thought to first use the term Wicca with two c?

Regardless of who were the first to use it though, Wicca with two c didn't appear until 1962, so a good decade after it was first founded.

By that time, Gardner had already been called "devil worshipper" by the press once or twice…

It's crucial to understand that time were different back then. The name Wicca, although an archaic word for witch/wizard ("wiccacraeft"), it sounded less offensive and dangerous to the broader public than if Gardner had continued calling this the "witch-cult". Simply by not calling it Witchcraft, he managed to attract people to it who might have otherwise been too scared or biased to explore it. Which is funny if you think that it's the same word, only an older version of it! And yet, it's understandable: this may not have been the Middle Ages anymore, but witchcraft was still illegal and had real ramifications for people who were accused of practicing. Truth be told, it still is, in many parts of the world. Going for the safer option was a smart move!

But there's also another reason we're calling ourselves Wicca: by using this older version of the word, it's like Wiccans are stating their intention to honor and continue old Pagan traditions.

So… does that make Wiccan less deserving of being taken seriously than people who call themselves witches or wizards? Definitely not.

"Don't mistake my kindness for weakness," as the song goes. Songs can be wise, can't they?

That being said, being a Wiccan and being a Witch are not always synonymous. We'll explain more in the next chapter, hang on to your broom dear one!

CHAPTER 3: ARE YOU A WICCAN OR A WITCH?

Now that we've seen what Wicca is (and isn't) all about, it's time for the tricky part.

Perhaps you've heard in your witchy circles people saying things like "I'm no Wiccan" (because they believe that being a Wiccan is somehow less than being a "real" Witch). Or, if you are new to all this, you've probably followed a few witchy accounts on Instagram or YouTube, to get inspiration. And at some point, you may have come across people talking about how being a Wiccan versus being a Witch and how the two are not the same…

Did that leave you super confused? After all, we did just say that Wicca is another word for Witchcraft, so what's the difference if any?

Patience, dear one. We will explain everything.

The difference between Wicca and Witchcraft is that the first is a religion (or spirituality, if you will) whereas the second is a practice. And as any kind of practice, it may also be tied to a religion or spirituality — or it may not. Below we will attempt to unpack this in a three-fold way: we'll see how not all Wiccans are Witches, how not all Witches are Wiccans and how you can be both, if you so desire!

NOT ALL WICCANS ARE WITCHES

When Gardner first started his "witch-cult" of his, the focus was mostly on rituals (many of which, as we've seen, were taken from Crowley's unique brand of ceremonial magick). Gardner's first acolytes and initiates were all deeply interested in the occult, most of them had a background in ceremonial magick from other secret organizations and were highly geared towards the practical aspects of the Craft; namely, raising power from the elements and deities and performing spells (although they didn't really call them "spells"). Sure, it was tightly knit with the worshipping part (which usually involved nudity and scourging) but the end goal was always to raise power to achieve a certain goal.

However, Wicca today is officially a religion — albeit one with an eclectic theology and no real central authority. As the people who practice Wicca now come from all corners of the world and from all sorts of different backgrounds, perhaps it will come as no surprise that not all of them are practicing witches.

What does that mean, practically?

Think of it as a luscious field, rich with flowers in full bloom: you may choose to walk among the flowers every day, rejoicing by their colors and fragrance, perhaps take a few photos or cut a few every now and then for your vases… but otherwise leave them be. Or you may choose to harvest the flowers: use their petals for teas and herb mixes; make soap or candles by combining them with essential oils; boil their stems for their medicinal properties; even dry them out and grind them into colorful dust you can use for your makeup! So many things one can do with flowers… At the end of the day though, the field is the same. The flowers are the same. It's just the way you choose to use them that changes — and the way you choose to use them, at the end of the day, boils down to what kind of person you are and what brings you the most joy.

Is it starting to become clearer now?

Simply enjoying the flowers doesn't make you a better or a worse person than the person who chooses to work with them. It just makes you, you.

It's the same thing with non-practicing Wiccans.

They can still reap the rewards of living a healthy life and happy, in tune with Nature and in communion with the gods and goddesses of their Pantheon. They can partake in the magickal energy all around us without having to work with it and shape it for specific results...

Want another analogy? Think about it as a party. (After all, Pagans know how to celebrate.)

Now, at this party, there will be alcohol offered freely. You can drink that alcohol and be merry... or you can use that alcohol to make intricate, sophisticated cocktails that you will then drink and be merry or even offer to others. It's basically the difference between a party goer and a mixologist: they're both going at the same party, it's just that the latter has a bit more work to do! And making cocktails can be their hobby, their way of meeting new people, their way of making a living or simply their way of keeping their wits sharp and learning new things!

Are we saying then that non-practicing Wiccans are lazy? Waiting on the practicing ones to do all the work? No. In fact, they both need each other.

At a (Christian) church, you have both the priest and the flock. At a piano recital, you have both the pianist and the audience. At a theater group, you have both the director and the actors. None of these groups of people are lesser than the others — they just have a different focus, discipline or specialization.

You don't have to be a virtuoso pianist or even know how to read the notes to enjoy music!

So what do non-practicing Wiccans do then, if they're not practicing magic? In a way, they do: they're practicing the rare and precious magic of living their lives to the fullest, with an open heart, a respect for Nature and with awe for the gifts each new day brings…

But seriously, non-practicing Wiccans are worshipping the Goddess and the God (in any variation they choose). The way they worship is still a matter of personal preference: some will pray twice a day and light candles, others will quietly smile every now and then, knowing their gods are with them. Most, will do both, depending on the day and how busy they are with other things! Yes, that's right, Wiccans also live in the mundane world, where bills need to be paid and loved ones (who may or may not be Wiccans as well) need to be nurtured...

Sometimes, they won't have time to do much. But as long as they're living their lives with the intention to never harm anyone and be happy, they're still enjoying those proverbial flowers in that field.

Not all Witches are Wiccans

Which brings us to the opposite end of that argument. As we've seen, people have been practicing witchcraft, in their own way, for many millennia. Definitely way before 2000 BCE (when, as we've seen in the first part of the book, we have the first written mention of practicing witchcraft in the Code of Hammurabi). And the way they've practiced witchcraft, has been as diverse as them — and always in conjunction with their local Pagan beliefs[21].

For example, someone who practiced witchcraft in ancient Africa, say in what we now know as the Yoruba tradition, didn't necessarily followed the same rituals and rules of conduct as someone who practiced witchcraft in ancient Mesopotamia or

---

[21] Leo Ruickbie, Witchcraft Out of the Shadows: A Complete History, Robert Hale; New edition (April 1, 2012).

ancient Scandinavia. Certainly though, there are certain broader methods of performing witchcraft that we know were used in many different cultures.

One of these methods is spellbinding: the art of imbuing an object (or a human being) with a specific intention — also known as "hex" when that intention was malevolent. Spellbinding could be done by carving symbols in a candle, a rock or a piece of wood; by tying ceremonial knots in a ribbon or a piece of cloth the "victim" of the spell would be wearing; by placing spelled objects in that person's vicinity; or simply, by chanting words and incantations.

Another is divination, the art of seeing the future. This also has been practiced in a variety of methods, across different cultures. (We'll talk all about it in the next part of the book!)

Another is spiritual communion: conjuring or communicating with non-corporeal beings that can either be ancestors' spirits (ghosts) or extra-dimensional beings (what people refer to as "demons", "angels" or even deities). This was done either to get help from the beings for problems to community was facing, or for selfish reasons such as to get revenge on one's enemies or inflict fear and amass power.

Healing, either achieved through energetical touch (what we would call "reiki" today) either through herbs, tinctures and poultices (through knowledge that we'd today call homeopathic or herbal remedies), has always been a big part of witchcraft as well. Healers were always revered and sought-after in ancient times, usually called things like "wise ones" or "white witches". Sometimes though, whether because they made a mistake or simply because an illness was too far gone for them to cure (or, in more rare cases, were sabotaging the treatment for their own gain), healers would get blamed by their communities and accused of everything from failing crops to contagious diseases.

Truth be told, most acts of magic are at their core neutral. They become "good" or "bad" based on the intention with which are yielded. In a way, magic is a bit like money: you can be a generous philanthropist or a ruthless billionaire that profits over other people's hard work. That doesn't mean money is inherently good or bad by itself, it depends on how you use it.

Historically, witchcraft has been associated with sacrifices. Most often animal sacrifices, but also human in some cases. It sounds horrible, I know! But does that make every sorcerer/practitioner who ever made a sacrifice "evil"? Not necessarily. You need to consider the historical era and the mindset around this. Human life, although cherished as a miracle in a collective level, on a personal level didn't mean as much as it did today — especially if we're talking about the life of someone who wasn't wealthy or powerful.

Sometimes, people truly believed that by sacrificing one human to appease the gods they could save their whole village... That doesn't make them evil, it just makes them tragically misinformed.

Sacrifice, in a way, is always necessary to create magick. You need to give something to get something, it may sound like the lyrics of an R'n'B song but it's actually true on a cosmic level as well. You can't create something out of nothing. That being said, a sacrifice doesn't have to involve spilling anyone's blood for the spell (any spell) to work: it can be an energetic sacrifice, a way of giving thanks and committing yourself to serve the energies/deities or a symbolic sacrifice (like cutting some of your hair, pouring wine or milk on the earth, or burying an object in the ground). Wiccans who practice magick understand that, as it is closely connected to the Wiccan Rede and the Wiccan law of doing no harm.

But not all people who practice witchcraft today are associated with Wicca or adhere to that law. People who follow Crowley's religion for instance, Thelema, believe that "the full of the law is do as thou wilt". Many non-European practitioners of witchcraft, for instance those who practice branches of Yoruba or Vodun, may include small animal sacrifices in their practices. Does that make them evil? If you believe that, dear one, then I hope you're not eating meat...

The point of this chapter is not to scare you off, but to show you that not all people adhere to the same moral codes. This applies to all aspects of life, as well as witchcraft. So when you meet a Witch, be mindful but also please be considerate: some people may even find it insulting to be confused with Wiccans, as they are very proud of their own magical traditions.

In the end, you should respect everyone you meet along this Path — but put your trust in the people who have earned it. That being said, it's not unheard of for Wiccan witches and non-Wiccan witches to work together or use each other's services. Especially in our day and age, when there are so many practitioners out there and you can access their services or merchandise online… That's not a bad thing.

As long as you're not hurting anyone, or hiring someone non-bound by the Wiccan Laws to do the hurting for you. For example, if you're a Wiccan, it's not okay to do a spell to "get back" on someone or put a hex on someone, and it's definitely not okay to pay a non-Wiccan to place that spell or hex for you. (That would be like saying you're a vegan and then paying someone to kill and eat animals in front of you, so that you get the satisfaction! No sane vegan would ever do that, as they're vehemently opposed to causing any animals harm…)

But as long as your motives are pure and your heart is open, then by all means, do mingle with your non-Wiccan, modern Pagan community. There are so many vibrant traditions out there and so many things to learn, dear one!

YOU CAN DEFINITELY BE BOTH A WICCAN AND A WITCH

So as we've seen, being a Wiccan and being a Witch are not mutually inclusive. Now it's time for the good news: they're not mutually exclusive either! You can totally be both a devout Wiccan and a badass witch, if that's what you want. How?

It's simple, dear one.

Just keep the Wiccan Law forever in your heart, whenever you practice spells or rituals. Make the "an it harm none" your internal moral compass that will help you navigate tricky situations or decide whether a specific ritual or a spell are a good fit for you. For example: if you practice divination as a Wiccan, and you're doing tarot readings for other people, you should refrain from answering questions that would motivate or empower people to hurt others.

(So, if a client asks you "how can I make my lover leave his wife" or "how can I make my rival at the office lose the promotions so that I get it myself", kindly explain that you cannot answer questions like that as they clash with your beliefs. Most people will understand,

and not persist. If they do persist, it's a sign they shouldn't be your clients anyway.)

But basically, that's your only limitation as a Wiccan Witch. If you're not hurting anyone (directly or indirectly), then there is no spell, ritual or practice that is out of your reach!

Here are some ways you can be a kickass Wiccan Witch:

-You can use the power of plants to help a loved one feel better or protect yourself and your home from bad energies.

-You can work with crystals to increase your psychic powers and intuition or augment the vibrations of your home.

-You can use cooking spells to whip up meals and confections that will make your loved ones happy, while at the same time protecting them from the inside.

-You can work with the Elements to protect yourself and your loved ones from anyone who would cause you harm or to manifest intentions that would help you live a better life.

-You can commune with plants and animals, to nurture them and help them grow and heal. In return, they can help you with your Craft, acting as familiars or omens.

-You can commune with spirits, of the ones who have passed or of ones you have a connection with, to gleam answers, get help or even help them find peace (although that's not recommended for beginners, you need to know what you're doing!)

-You can work with your sisters and brothers to raise a collective power to help Mother Earth heal or protect your homeland in case of emergencies (hey, if it worked for the coven Gardner witnessed trying to protect Brittain from Nazi invaders...).

-You can work with everything from plants and crystals to divination and deities in order to nurture your relationship and enhance a loving atmosphere at home. (Be careful though: this does not mean creating something that does exist, making someone fall in love with you or tying someone energetically to you even if they want out... This will surely backfire!)

-You can use all these tools mentioned above to heal yourself, physically and emotionally and enjoy your life more.

-You can get in tune with the waxing and waning phases of the Moon, to help things grow in your life or let go of things that are holding you back.

-You can protect yourself from people who mean you harm, from people who soak up your energy or from places that have a bad aura.

Does that sound exciting, dear one? Are you eager to get started? Of course you are!

This is what this next part of the book is all about. On Part 3: Everyday Magick, we'll get acquainted with all the basic tools and rituals you're gonna need to have in your arsenal, as you get started on your witchy Path. We'll then dig a little deeper on the different ways to practice witchcraft, so that you find the one that better speaks to your personality (along with a few go-to magickal tips for each type). Then, as promised, we'll talk about divination and tarot cards and help you get started with your first divination readings. Once we've covered all that, it's time for some seasonal spells and getting you better acquainted with the Sabbats and Esbats — and what kind of magickal energies abound in each one...

Bear in mind, dear one, that this is just the tip of the iceberg. If you're serious about your Path, you'll never start learning and growing. You'll get back to the same spells, change the words or some of the ingredients; you'll come up with new ways to do tarot readings; you'll start new Sabbat traditions of your own. As you know, us Pagans are infamous for doing things our own way! So please, don't feel the need to treat the book as the ultimate authority: the ultimate authority is you. If something described here (or in any book) doesn't feel right to you, then trust your gut. As long as you're not hurting anyone, of course!

(Disclaimer: You won't find any spells or rituals in this book that break the Wiccan Law of "do no harm". We're kosher that way. Sorry... but not really sorry, why would you want to do harm?)

Okay, that's it. Enough about theory and history lessons. Although of course they had their usefulness and brought you were you needed to be and develop a sense of understanding, now it's time for the real fun to begin!

PART 3: EVERYDAY MAGICK

Chapter 1: Basic Tools and Rituals

Welcome to the third and final part of this book, dear one!

They do say all good things come in threes, don't they? Yes, they do, especially when "they" are Wiccans. After all, "Mind the Threefold Laws you should, three times bad and three times good," according to our Wiccan Rede[22]!

---

[22] "The Wiccan Rede" (Full Version) as depicted in The Celtic Connection website, https://wicca.com/celtic/wicca/rede.htm

So if you're itching for some magick and practical knowledge, this part of the book has your back. We'll start

CHOOSE THE TOOLS THAT WORK FOR YOU

We've all seen those vintage images of witches riding their brooms, dressed all in black, a tall conical hat on their heads and a black cat on their tails…

A quick scroll on Instagram today, reveals a slightly (but not a lot) different image of what it means to be a witch: we see women with long, flowy hair somewhere in the woods, surrounded by cauldrons, wands, crystals (so.many.crystals), tarot cards, pendants, altars, herb jars and gourds, spellbooks, skulls and feathers, candles… Did we mention cauldrons?

Do you really need to go to Diagon Alley with a full list, like Harry and his friends before school season at Hogwarts, to be able to call yourself a witch? No, not really. In fact, every single one of the tools we'll discuss in this chapter as "basic", you could substitute for just your brilliant mind and your strong intention to manifest your desires! So why then, bother with objects at all?

It's not about capitalism or consumerism (although of course, it doesn't hurt to support small, independent witchy creators). It's mostly about your psychology. See, when you're first getting started on your witchy Path, it's only natural to *want to look the part*. You have all this self-doubt creeping in, that impostor syndrome whispering in your ear that "there's no such thing as real magick, you're just pretending", that gnawing fear that you don't really have what it takes or that you wouldn't even know where to begin… It can all be overwhelming, dear one.

That's where all these tools come in.

When you don't trust yourself and the power of your own heart and mind as well as the power of Nature (where witchcraft truly resides), these tools and objects will help you get into the zone and relieve some of the pressure: you may not fully trust yourself yet, but somehow you trust in them. Like talismans, magickal tools and objects give you something tangible to focus on. Something to hold on your hands, something to look at, something to smell or even something to taste. It's much easier than just looking at a blank wall…

Think of it as painting. It is known that, to create great abstract paintings, you first need to know how to sketch in a naturalistic way. That's exactly what Pablo Picasso did: his early sketches of birds, when he first went to art school, were so realistic you thought they would fly away! But when he grew into his art, he created the cubist, abstract forms he's become famous for.

Like Picasso, you too need to learn the rules in order to be able to break them or realize you never really needed them in the first place...

So, without further ado, here are your witchy essentials to get your started!

Book of Shadows

Ah, the Book of Shadows! You've seen it in TV shows, from the 90's Charmed to its recent reboot and everything in between... You know how it's supposed to look like by now: old, sturdy, with a leather cover in a dark color, a pentacle or a tricerta (more on sacred symbols later) engraved in the front, containing precious spells... But given that you're not a legacy witch and you didn't accidentally find one in your attic, how do you go about acquiring one? Can you just buy it on Amazon or Etsy?

Yes you can — but please don't.

The Book of Shadows is supposed to be your depository of spells and witchy knowledge. If you are not a legacy witch, then it's supposed to start with you, grow and evolve as you grow and evolve. So in the beginning, your Book of Shadows can just be a nice, blank notebook! It doesn't have to be expensive, or contain any magickal symbols (although of course, if you find one that you absolutely love how it looks, you should go ahead and buy it). In fact, it's considered a much better practice if you make your Book of Shadows yourself.

You can start with a plain notebook in a color that speaks to your Craft: it can be black or brown, sure, but it can also be white, purple, grey, green, gold… as long as it's a color that speaks to you and makes you want to spend time with it! It's better that you don't buy it online, either. Spend some time in an actual bookstore, touch some notebooks: see if any of them makes your hands tingle or if you have a gut feeling about a particular one. It doesn't matter how it looks, you can always customize it later.

Got your notebook? Great! Now, to make it into your Book of Shadows.

As with every new item you buy to use into your Craft (or any second-hand items of clothing or furniture you purchase), you'll first need to purify it; to make sure there are no lingering negative energies on it. To give it a clean slate, energetically speaking! So go ahead and purify it.

(We'll explain more about purifying in the next part, about rituals.)

Then, you can decorate your Book's cover and back with symbols that speak to you. This can be anything from the Pentacle to the triple moon symbol, to the alchemical symbols for the Elements.

You can even press flowers or glue crystals onto it. Just let your imagination soar!

Once you're happy with how it looks, it's time to start writing in it.

Traditionally, the first thing you should write in the first page is your name (your given name, or the name you've chosen for yourself as a Witch) and the date when you decided to start following your Path. Then, depending on which specific pantheon or deities you feel a closer connection to, you can also dedicate your Book of Shadows to Them.

If you identify as a Wiccan, it would be an excellent idea to copy the full version of the Wiccan Rede on the second or third page. There are a few different versions of the Wiccan Rede available online, but perhaps the most commonly used is featured on the official website of wicca.com. Feel free to visit their website and look for it yourself[23], or find it here:

The Wiccan Rede

Bide within the Law you must, in perfect Love and perfect Trust.

Live you must and let to live, fairly take and fairly give.

---

[23] "The Wiccan Rede" (Full Version) as depicted in The Celtic Connection website, https://wicca.com/celtic/wicca/rede.htm

For tread the Circle thrice about to keep unwelcome spirits out.

To bind the spell well every time, let the spell be said in rhyme.

Light of eye and soft of touch, speak you little, listen much.

Honor the Old Ones in deed and name,

let love and light be our guides again.

Deosil go by the waxing moon, chanting out the joyful tune.

Widdershins go when the moon doth wane,

and the werewolf howls by the dread wolfsbane.

When the Lady's moon is new, kiss the hand to Her times two.

When the moon rides at Her peak then your heart's desire seek.

Heed the North winds mighty gale, lock the door and trim the sail.

When the Wind blows from the East, expect the new and set the feast.

When the wind comes from the South, love will kiss you on the mouth.

When the wind whispers from the West, all hearts will find peace and rest.

Nine woods in the Cauldron go, burn them fast and burn them slow.

Birch in the fire goes to represent what the Lady knows.

Oak in the forest towers with might, in the fire it brings the God's Insight. Rowan is a tree of power causing life and magick to flower.

Willows at the waterside stand ready to help us to the Summerland.

Hawthorn is burned to purify and to draw faerie to your eye.

Hazel-the tree of wisdom and learning adds its strength to the bright fire burning.

White are the flowers of Apple tree that brings us fruits of fertility.

Grapes grow upon the vine giving us both joy and wine.

Fir does mark the evergreen to represent immortality seen.

Elder is the Lady's tree burn it not or cursed you'll be.

Four times the Major Sabbats mark in the light and in the dark.

As the old year starts to wane the new begins, it's now Samhain.

When the time for Imbolc shows watch for flowers through the snows.

When the wheel begins to turn soon the Beltane fires will burn.

As the wheel turns to Lamas night power is brought to magick rite.

Four times the Minor Sabbats fall use the Sun to mark them all.

When the wheel has turned to Yule light the log the Horned One rules.

In the spring, when night equals day time for Ostara to come our way.

When the Sun has reached it's height time for Oak and Holly to fight.

Harvesting comes to one and all when the Autumn Equinox does fall.

Heed the flower, bush, and tree by the Lady blessed you'll be.

Where the rippling waters go cast a stone, the truth you'll know.

When you have and hold a need, harken not to others greed.

With a fool no season spend or be counted as his friend.

Merry Meet and Merry Part bright the cheeks and warm the heart.

Mind the Three-fold Laws you should three times bad and three times good.

When misfortune is enow wear the star upon your brow.

Be true in love this you must do unless your love is false to you.

These Eight words the Rede fulfill:

"An Ye Harm None, Do What Ye Will"

Isn't it beautiful, dear one? But if you choose not to copy paste the full version, just make sure to write the Wiccan Law, "An Ye Harm None, Do What Ye Will".

That's the most important part after all!

Okay, now that you have your Book of Shadows purified, adorned and inscribed, it's time to begin using it. How do you do that? There are many ways:

-You can start by writing down spells, as you learn them.

-You can write the meanings of tarot cards (you'll find them in the next chapters!) or design your tarot spreads.

-You can write about your dreams, if you felt were prophetic, and return to that page later to see if something came about.

-You can make pages for all the major Wiccan celebrations, include rituals for these celebrations and seasonal spells and prayers.

-You can create a table of correspondences for the rest of your tools (as in, what each color stands for, what you should be using each crystaf for etc), so that you have everything at hand.

-You can write prayers for the Goddess and the God.

-You can draw Pentacles as mandalas (draw them without thinking, as you meditate on things).

-You can write recipes for magickal foods, elixirs or potions.

-You can write your desires, how you would ideally want your life to evolve, what are your intentions for this part of your journey... Feel free to revisit and adapt this part later on!

Your Book of Shadows should be private to you and kept somewhere safe. Think of it like your journal: you wouldn't want people to go about reading your journal, would you, dear one?

Altar

Just like your Book of Shadows is your journal, your altar is your witchy office: the place where you'll do your worshipping, your spell casting, your divination practicing... Of course like everything else on this list, you don't necessarily need an altar: your whole house can be your altar — or your nearest grove, forest or beach (see more on Nature, later in this chapter). But having a specific space just for you, where you can get your witchy vibes on, it will be very inspiring and liberating, especially at first.

So, your altar then. It really depends on your living arrangements: how discreet you need it to be (if say, you have roommates that are not exactly into the occult), how big of a space it can take.

An altar can be anything from a desk, to a shelf, to a side table — even a cupboard or a chest that you can keep closed when there are prying eyes about! There's no steadfast rule on what your altar should be made from either, but it's best to choose natural ingredients like wood or a flat stone surface. Remember to purify it before you start using it!

If you look for the hashtag #altar on Instagram, you'll find close to one million posts that could help you get inspired on what your own altar could look like... but remember that there are no set "rules" about what you should include or not. Only guidelines, and your best judgement.

Traditionally, on your altar you can have any statues or symbols of deities you worship (if you're eclectic in your beliefs, this could also include a statue of Buddha or Madonna). You can have your Book of Shadows, your tarot card decks (or any other divination methods you use) and your candles. It's also considered a good idea to include representations of the Elements and place them in the appropriate Directions:

-a pentacle, a rock, a crystal, a plant or a green candle for Earth (North)

-a bell, a feather, an athame or a yellow candle for Air (East)

-a wand, a cauldron or an orange/red candle for Fire (South)

-a chalice, a small jar filled with salt water, a sea shell or a blue candle for Water (West)

-a statue of a deity or a white or purple candle for Spirit (Center)

(We'll talk a bit more about the Elements, their Directions and further correspondences on the next part about rituals.)

Wondering what some of these things mentioned above are and how to use them? Let's go through the rest of the list of your essential tools and you're find out!

Cauldron

Perhaps one of the most "cliche" tools associated with witchcraft out there. How many times have you seen witches in anything from paintings to Shakespearean plays, stirring potions in a bubbling cauldron? And usually the ingredients they keep adding are quite elaborate… Who has the time to find "eye of newt" in this day and age? Definitely not a Wiccan who would never use the body parts of an animal so flippantly!

Energetically, a cauldron symbolizes transformation through fire; rebirth. You don't actually have to boil anything in it (depending on where you live it may not even be safe to do so): you can just use it as a safe place to have your tea lights and candles and experiment with adding spices and herbs to them as they burn.

Athame

In sharp contrast to the cauldron, athames are actually not publicized enough: not many people who are not actually practicing witchcraft know about them. (Perhaps it's better that way?)

An athame is a ceremonial knife, usually with a white handle (made of ivory or bone). There are athames you can buy online, or you can use any hand-carved old knife, as long as you purify it.

Very important: you're not supposed to use your Athame to cut anything physical, so please don't use a knife you use for cooking or eating! Athames are symbolical "cutting cords" and redirecting energies: you can use them to carve symbols on candles, create pentacles on air or basically use them as you would use a wand. In fact, most witches prefer athames from wands, as their sharp edge is a better conduit for energy than the blunt edge of any wand.

Speaking of which...

Wand

I know, dear one. Wands are cool and bring out your Harry Potter fan...

But contrary to popular belief, you don't actually need a wand. The wand is you, your arm or your fingers (or your athame). Despite that fact, many witches choose to have wands on their altars, as they are a good symbol of power, fertility, masculine energy (it is a phallic symbol after all) and they represent the element of Fire when you are not able to have something flammable around.

When it comes to choosing your wand: please don't buy it online.

The best thing you can do is take a walk in the woods or find a fallen branch somewhere. Carve the branch yourself, to the size and shape it feels right: you can add symbols, hang ribbons or attach crystals to it... It needs to feel comfortable and warm in your hand when you hold it!

You can use your wand in spell casting, in creating Pentacles on air (just like your athame) or to perform a symbolic Rite that combines masculine and feminine energy, by placing your wand inside your Chalice.

Chalice

The chalice symbolizes the Element of Water in your Altar, as well as feminine energy.

Any cup, glass or mug can be your chalice — although traditionally, it needs to be made from clear materials that reflect the light, like glass or crystal.

You can use your chalice to sip wine or water in ceremonies, to purify water and crystals or even to contain your runes, flowers, sea shells or anything else that brings to mind femininity!

Pentacle

We've been talking about Pentacles a lot, haven't we? And for good reason: a Pentacle is to Wiccans what the Star of David is to a Jew or the Holy Cross to a Christian. It's a manifestation of divine energy and a reminder of the things we believe in the most.

The Pentacle is practically a five-point star inside a circle. It is created to contain all five Elements: Earth, Air, Fire, Water and Spirit, each one represented in one of the star's five points. The circle symbolizes the World (both Above and Below). What the Pentacle is saying in plain English is that everything is contained within this world: all the elements, as well as Divine Spirit, all working together as part of the same grand design...

In slightly less philosophical terms, the pentacle is a super strong symbol of protection. Many witches and Wiccans have it engraved on the altar, or crafted from stone or wood. Some choose to wear it as a necklace (or a tattoo). In your altar it also symbolizes the element of Earth.

A silver bell

Also known as "the voice of the Goddess", a silver bell can be a beautiful way to ground yourself and meditate at the beginning and the end of a ritual. It's considered to clear the energies, and accentuate your intentions — very much like ringing a bell brings the students back to the classroom or announces guests at your home!

You can experiment with how many times you ring the bell, as each number is considered to bring about different energies. (We'll get more into numbers later on.)

In your altar it symbolizes the element of Air.

Candles

Candles are probably the simplest form of magick — so simple, they're even used in mainstream Christianity! Think about it: what is lighting a candle to pray if not a spell of sorts?

Candle magick is such an extensive field, it would require its own book. I urge you to find books on candle magick and read up, dear one!

At this point, what you need to know about candles is that similar to the bell, they can clear the energy of a space (immediately purify it) and they can also carry your intentions on their flames, sending it from the earth up to the sky as the smoke rises...

You can use candles to honor your deities or ancestors; to meditate before or during a ritual; to celebrate a particular Pagan holiday; to carve symbols or intentions and burn them as spells. Once you figure out what color to use for each occasion (consult the part about colors later on), you can use for everything from love spells to divination and fertility spells. You can use your athame to carve runes, names or symbols on their shaft; you can burn small pieces of paper (as symbols of things you want to let go of); you can place them on top of effigies (as symbols of things you want to keep burning bright); you can drip their wax to seal your intentions or spells.

Just remember to be safe and always put them out afterwards! When you do, remember to thank them as you blow — they deserve it, candles are the most hard-working witchy tools!

Crystals

Crystals are pretty. They're also powerful and healing — if you know how to use them properly.

The problem with crystals however, is that you don't really know where they came from: how exactly they were mined and if the people who mined them were exploited or given a fair wage... As a Wiccan who believes in not harming anyone, directly or indirectly, you need to be mindful of these things. It's better to buy crystals only locally, and when possible from people who were directly involved in mining them.

That being said, crystal magick is another extensive field you can look into if you want: there's practically a crystal for any kind of energy you'd like to emulate[24]!

---

[24] Scott Cunningham, (1987), Cunningham's Encyclopedia of Crystal, Gem, and Metal Magic.

To begin with, here are some crystals you can start experimenting with:

-clear quartz, for clarity, spirituality and intuition

-rose quartz, for love, happiness and affection

-amethyst, for protection, wisdom and intuition

-selenite, for intuition, psychic powers and divination

-pyrite, for power, courage and protection

-black onyx, for honesty, power and protection

Crystals on your altar usually symbolize Earth, but depending on their properties they can symbolize other elements as well. You can use them as energetical batteries, to charge your tarot cards, your Book of Shadows or spells; you can carry them with you for protection; you can place them around your house for protection and good vibes; you can use them to sanctify the water on your chalice. Some witches take that last part one step further and like to bathe with their crystals in the bathtub — but that doesn't really do anything besides looking cool on Instagram and pissing the crystals off.

Because yeah, your crystals have personalities and they don't like being mistreated. You should also remember to charge them every now and then: place them on a window sill so that they can get fresh energy from the sun or the moonlight.

Plants, herbs, flowers and essential oils

Every flower and plant out there has some magickal (and medicinal) properties that can help you with your Craft. This is also a field that you may end up studying your whole life and still discover new properties by trial and error. You can use herbs to burn as incense (see also the next part about sage); you can brew plants and flowers for teas and potions; you can include plants and herbs in cooking spells; you can anoint your candles or your skin with essential oils that bring out a specific quality...

There really is no boundaries to the things you can use your herbal arsenal for!

Scott Cunningham, one of the greatest writers of Wicca, has written an excellent book about the magickal abilities of plants that should be part of every witch's book collection[25]. But just as a quick

---

[25] Scott Cunningham, (1985) Cunningham's Encyclopedia of Magical Herbs.

reference, here are some popular, easy to find and safe to use plants you can start including in your witchy repertoire:

-basil, for love, wealth and protection

-rosemary, for protection, healing and love

-rose, for passion, love and luck

-cinnamon, for success, healing and love

-jasmin, for love, money and prophetic dreams

-sage, for wisdom, banishment of negative energies and protection

-mugwort, for astral projection and prophetic dreams

-lavender, for serenity, peace and a good night's sleep

Salt, sage and palo santo

We've already seen how sage can be used to banish negative energies. In shamanic traditions of Native Americans, they'd use to burn sage to purify the air or someone who may be carrying negative energies. Modern witches and Wiccans use sage to protect and purify, along with salt and palo santo. As a general rule, sage tends to remove all vibrations, both positive and negative, reinstating an energetic clean slate.

But as far as protection and purification goes, salt is perhaps the strongest of them all. (Those superstitions about throwing salt over your shoulder or creating a salt circle to keep ghosts out of a room have been popular for a reason.) No bad energy can break through a salt circle or a salt bath. You can purify your tools, from your Book of Shadows to your candles and crystals by burying them in salt for a while (from a few seconds to a whole night or more, depending on the situation). You can also just sprinkle a bit of salt around your altar, or carry a few grains of salt in your pockets (or place them with some lavender under your pillow to ward off nightmares).

Palo santo is a gentler alternative, as it does not remove any positive vibrations, only the negative ones. For extraordinary results, you can combine all three.

Broom (yes, really)

You're not going to use it for flying, please don't try. Now that we've gotten this out of the way, brooms can be used to energetically clean your space and ward off malevolent spirits. Traditionally they're called "besoms".

Keep your besom in a corner facing your front door, for good luck.

Yarn and ribbons

Knot magick is a very interesting field. The idea behind it is that you can meditate and tie knots on a ribbon or yarn to remove obstacles or manifest your intentions. (That's more or less how prayer beads and worry beads came to be!)

Many witches always have ribbons in all colors at the ready, to use depending on the occasion and the spell. You can also hang them in your hair or in your house, for protection.

As for yarn, you can use it to make your own "Witch's Belt", also called a Cingulum. Basically you need to take eight yarn colors, one to represent each Sabbat and Esbat and you slowly braid them together throughout the year: you start with the ribbons of the first three Sabbats and Esbats until you have a braid, then you create two more braids as the following celebrations come... and in the end you braid all three braids together.

The Cingulum is to be worn as a belt over your ceremonial robes to amplify your power, but many Witches also choose to wear it wrapped around their wrists as a bracelet as well.

Ceremonial robes

Yes, we said "ceremonial robes". But they definitely don't have to be black, or like a Halloween costume. Your "robes" can basically be anything from a loose, comfortable long dress, to flowy yoga pants and a shirt if you're less into the theatrics. It's nice if it touches the earth, as it provides you with a tangible connection between Above and Below, but the most important thing is that you feel clean, special and comfortable when wearing them! For that reason, it's better to have a particular type of clothing you only use for your Craft and not for your everyday life.

Many witches (especially ones that follow Gardner's practice) will work their Craft naked, however this may not always be the most practical or viable option!

Nature

Yes, Nature is your ultimate tool. Being a Witch is all about understanding and living according to Natural Law. In fact, Nature could easily replace most of your tools mentioned here.

For starters, when you're out in Nature you don't need representations of the Elements to work with; you are literally surrounded by them! You can take water from a running stream, a lake or the sea; you can get barefoot and dig your toes on the ground or in the sand to draw energy from the earth; you can recharge by spreading your hands open wide towards the light of the Sun of the Moon; if you want to redirect energy, fallen branches can be your wand; if you're near the ocean, the salt of the water works as a protection shield and a natural purificator.

Just be careful with lighting a fire in Nature. Do it respectfully, safely and always put it out afterwards.

UNDERSTAND YOUR BASIC RITUALS

Okay, dear one, now you've got your tools at the ready. So... how do you go about using them?

There is literally no end to the rituals and spells you can start practicing daily with these tools. But first you need to master a few simple rituals that will serve as the basis you can build upon.

Meditation

Meditation is truly a witch's best friend — although we may not always have called it that.

The practice of meditation was first recorded in the Vedas around 1500 BCE (see the first part of the book for more info on the Vedas) and was well developed in Taoist China and Buddhist India around 600 BCE. In the Western world, meditation (in the form we know it today) became popular around the 1960s-70s, as part of the renewed interest in the occult and in oriental wisdom. But the thing is, witches always meditated. They may have called it "stepping between the worlds" or "opening up their Sight" or simply spending time alone in Nature, but the premise remains the same: to be able to tap your inner Power, first you must quiet your mind.

There are currently many great apps in the market that can help you turn meditation into a daily practice but perhaps you don't need them. Try lighting a candle and just sitting for a while, looking at the flame and focusing on breathing calmly. Let the world around you slowly melt and disappear. You'll notice that with time, it will become easier to slip in and out of this deep state of mind — and it's a state of mind (or, non-mind) you need if you're to do any work on your Craft.

Purification

We touched upon this briefly in the previous part about tools: purification is a very important ritual that can be performed on anything from witchy and non-witchy objects to people and spaces. To purify something you need tools such as: salt, sage, palo santo, water and fire (and sometimes, crystals).

There are many purification techniques, depending on the situation:

-You can take a purifying shower (or stand out in the rain for a few seconds), letting the water wash away any lingering negative energies and feel your body being returned to a state of infinite possibility and power.

-You can burn a sage bundle or a palo santo stick, and smudge yourself, an object or your home. It is common to move your hand around in such a way that you create shapes with the smoke, usually Pentacles or the symbol of infinity (looks like the number 8 lying down).

-You can place the object, or your hands, in a bowl full of salt for a few moments or minutes. Let the Earth work its magick.

-You can, carefully, place the object or your hands over the flame of a candle — high enough so that you don't get burned, obviously! The idea is that the element of Fire will purify and transform any lingering negativity to new, vibrant energy.

-You can place some sage leaves on your chalice and fill it with water. Let the water sit for a while and the leaves to be soaked in. Then you can use this water to purify yourself or objects. (A little here will go a long way: just dip your fingers on the sanctified water and use them to tap some of it on your third-eye chakra, or on the object you want to purify.)

While performing any of these rituals, you can chant something like "remove the negativity of yesterday, bring only good vibes this way".

The words don't matter that much, use words that come naturally to you. It's the intention that counts, and your intention should be to purify this object or yourself.

Raising Power

Raising Power is like supercharging yourself with energy, so that you can redirect that energy towards the spell or ritual you're performing — or even towards that part of your body that is hurting or that area of your life that could use some improving.

Raising Power is much easier done with more witches, by joining hands and forming a circle. (With more people, it's easier to raise more energy and redirect it towards big threats, such as the amazon forest fires or wars and famine.) But if you're a solitary practitioner as so many of us are, you still have some very powerful allies you can work with to raise Power for your spells and rituals! Who are these amazing allies? The Elements.

Earth

The element of home and stability, the one that keeps you grounded and helps you find your True North. Earth is a great element to work with for spells/rituals that involve matters of home/career/finances.

Air

The element of inspiration and communication, of change and renewal. Always look in the East when working with Air. A great element to work with when you want to get a message across, or for matter that involve writing/talking to people/social life/traveling/studying.

Fire

The element of passion, creativity, sex and jest for life. Fire, residing in the direction of the South, is a great Element to invoke for sexual spells, but also anything that has to do with work projects you are passionate about or with spells to reclaim your power.

Water

The element of love, emotions, sensitivity; of surrendering and letting go. Water resides in the direction of the West and will be your perfect ally for anything from love and fertility spells/rituals to work on divination and healing.

Spirit

The element that binds them all together, existing in the Center, simultaneously inside and outside this world. Use spirit in protection rituals, to invoke deities or to bring your other spells/rituals full circle and give thanks.

Whenever you want to work with a specific energy/element, the simplest way to do so is to turn your body to face its Direction and light a candle in its honor. But it's considered a better idea, at least in the beginning, to combine all the elements (in the order that were mentioned here) moving clockwise in a circle with one of your arms extended — you can use a wand, an athame, a sage bundle or just your finger.

Once your ceremony/spell is over, do the same thing anti-clockwise to give thanks and release the energies/elements.

Invoking the Deities

How do you invoke a god/goddess?

This is a complicated matter and you should only embark on it once you feel comfortable that you understand and respect what this god/goddess is all about. Otherwise, at best nothing will happen and at worst you're risking making some deity annoyed...

So please, do your research, find the god/goddess you identify the most with or feel closer to (these are often called Patron or Matron deities) and develop a relationship with them — don't just call on them when you need something! Worship them during your daily life as well, send them love, light candles in their names and give them offerings. The same way a devout Christian would think about his or her favorite Saint, or about Jesus and God themselves.

Once you know what you're doing and who you're doing it with (and why), make your invocation with a clear, steady voice and state your intention. Use their formal names, or the names they have been called by their worshippers (for instance, Odin, is also called the AllFather). Mention the realms in which they rule and the areas of life they can affect them most.

Don't expect something to happen instantly. Sit with the intention for a while, meditating on the presence of your Patron or Matron deity. After a while, give thanks and release them.

It's only good manners, dear one!

Protection

Throughout your spells and rituals, you'll need to make sure you are protected from any negative energies from within, but also any restless spirits that make venture to enter from without. Creating a circle with the power of the Elements works as a protection shield, but you can also create a literal circle with a rope or salt on the ground and step inside it.

A smart and convenient way to always be protected is to purify a piece of jewelry (preferably silver or containing crystals) and invoke the Elements and deities to bless this jewelry and imbue it with Power. Then, you can wear it or hang it from your doorstep (or over your bed) whenever you want to feel safe and protected.

Chapter 2: Find Your Witchy Flavor

What kind of Witch are you? No, this is not a Buzzfeed quiz, it's a serious question.

In a similar way that doctors can be general practitioners or specialize in a particular field of medicine field (like oncology or gynaecology), you can decide to be a Witch that tries a bit of everything... of find your specific witchy flavor. Although finding that (and polishing it) will be your lifelong Journey, in this chapter you can get a brief understanding of the most prominent witch types — at least the ones that do not violate the Wiccan Law of doing no harm.

Elemental Witch

In a way, we're all Elemental Witches. We all need the Elements, especially Spirit, to draw Power from. But an elemental witch usually has a special connection to one of the elements — and that affects her Craft.

For example: have you always felt an affinity for fire? Do you find it easy manipulating candle flames with your energy or mind? That may be a sign that you're an Elemental Witch. Be careful though: the Elements are very powerful and you'll need to learn to control yourself around them because accidents do happen. (I once knew a Witch with an affinity for Water who managed to accidentally flood her apartment… twice!) You need to remember to balance yourself and your surroundings so, for instance, if Fire is strong within you, make sure you're surrounded by calming waters often.

Sea Witch

A sea witch is in a way an Elemental Witch with an affinity for Water — but her Power is supercharged by the ocean. Did you always feel a connection to the sea and the waves? When you're in a bad mood, do you find it easier to heal when you're by the oceanside? Has swimming or diving always felt like second nature to you and you've never felt any fear towards sea creatures? You may be a Sea Witch! It would be worth exploring the lore of supernatural creatures with ties to the ocean, like mermaids or selkies — you never know what you may discover about yourself!

GREEN WITCH

Another denomination of an Elemental Witch, this time with an affinity for Earth. Green witches have what we call "green thumbs": they're most at their element in the woods or at their garden, helping plants, flowers and trees grow and flourish. A green witch's home can start resembling a jungle after a while, once all her herbs are repotted and her flowers have bloomed…

Does that sound like you? Great! Being a Green Witch is a very useful skill and one our planet desperately needs!

KITCHEN WITCH

Kitchen (or hearth/home) witches are basically a Green Witch's close cousin. You too have an affinity for all earthy things and love working with plants and herbs — only you prefer the comfort of your own home and the warmth of your stove to the woods. A Kitchen Witch uses her Craft to nurture her loved ones through food, pays special attention to pets and kids and turns even simple tasks like cleaning the floor to opportunities for magick.

Hedge Witch

This is a term that's been thrown out a lot. It has taken to mean "a witch with no official training, mostly doing her own thing[26]" but traditionally, hedge witches are thought to exist a bit "in between". To cross over the "hedge" between the worlds and visit the realm of spirits. If you ever had experiences in the astral plane or it's always been easier for you to see spirits and interact with them, you may be a hedge witch.

Tip: if you are a hedge witch, please make sure to double down on your protection. Use every tool available to you to make sure no destructive spirits will ever "catch a ride" with you, okay?

---

[26] Mandy Mitchell, (2014) Hedgewitch Book of Days: Spells, Rituals, and Recipes for the Magical Year, Weiser Books.

Tech Witch

This is a new category, but one that's gaining ground. A tech witch understands that technology runs on electrical currents and magnetic energy and can use these energies to her benefit. Have you always been particularly lucky around electronics (that may not have been working properly for other people but always work for you)? Do you always manage to find internet even when the people next to you are struggling? Do you feel "seen" by the apps you download? You may be a tech witch!

Divination Witch

Every type of witch, even the ones who are not featured here (because they violate the Wiccan Law of doing no harm), usually practices some kind of divination. But a true divination witch usually has some kind of inherent foresight — either in the form of dreams or in the form of interpreting omens that come her way.

Divination is a fascinating field that everyone can learn and benefit from. In the next chapter, we'll talk in depth about it!

Chapter 3: Divination 101

Ah, to gaze upon the future and get answers on what's to come!

Admit it, dear one: you couldn't wait for this chapter to arrive.

(Perhaps you even skipped a couple of chapters to get here? Hopefully you didn't. There's much to learn in those chapters as well.)

Divination has been a companion of witches and Pagans since the beginning of time. The word itself, deriving from Latin, means both to "be inspired by a god" and to "foresee, foretell". In the ancient Pagan world, seers or "manteis" (in Greek) were revered and their counsel sought after, from both kings and commoners. Very often, seers would be brought onto the battlefield, to read the omens. That could mean either looking out for any incidents like birds flying or the clouds dissipating that could be interpreted as positive or negative, or sacrificing animals and studying their entrails for hidden messages from the gods. In many cases, a general would not attack unless they got the "go" from their seers. (Sometimes these seers would lie, having been bought by the opposing forces.)

If seers interpreted signs, oracles were thought to commune with the gods directly. The most famous oracle of the ancient world was the Oracle of Delphi, in Greece. In fact, it was once considered "the navel of the Earth" because of the importance that was placed in the prophecies Pythia (the priestess of the god Apollo who operated the oracle) would deliver to people. There is no clear verdict among historians on how these prophecies were given: some said she would inhale the vapors that emerged from a chasm between the rock and reach a state of lucid dreaming; others claimed she communed directly with the gods and spoke in tongues, or in obscure poetry verses. Most, however, agree that her prophecies were enigmatic — and have been interpreted differently by different people more than once, usually with dire consequences.

Consider this a cautionary tale, dear one.

When you start asking questions about the future, the answers may not come in the form you expect. You need to be prepared to read between the lines and think outside the box.

It wasn't just ancient Greece though that relied heavily on divination. From the Aztecs who worshipped Tezcatlipoca, the god of sorcerers and magic, to the Ifá divination system of the Yoruba that required an initiated priest/priestess called Awo, giving insights on the future and the will of the gods was a fundamental part of Pagan life. Seers would study animal entrails but also the movements of living animals, natural phenomena such as clouds and thunder, liquids such as coffee or tea, parts of the human body (like the palm of your hand or your iris) or use tools such as rocks, runes, cards and bamboo sticks. They would also gaze upon reflective surfaces such as mirrors or river streams or study the flames and the embers of a fire…

Anything, really, can be used as a divination tool — and it probably has been.

Of course, divination was officially forbidden in the early days of Christianity in Europe, along with all other Pagan practices, but that didn't mean people ever stopped using it. In fact, it's kinda forbidden in many countries even to this day — and yet divination practices are actually booming. All you have to do is log into Instagram and you'll come across anything from tarot cards and runes to people reading tea leaves and palms.

But where does it really come from? Can tea leaves actually tell us the future?

It doesn't work exactly like that, dear one.

To practice any kind of divination, you need to open yourself to messages — both from your subconscious and from the spirits and deities. You need to bring yourself to a state that's both focused and relaxed, almost meditative — but sometimes it can also work wonders to be under the influence of substances (not that we're advising that). That's what Pythia was doing after all, when she was inhaling those "vapors" back in ancient Greece… But maybe don't tell your professors at school that!

Ultimately, how you'll practice divination is, like many things in the Pagan world, a matter of personal preference. So if slaughtering a lamb and studying its entrails is not exactly your cup of tea (pun intended) keep reading: you'll find some of the most common divination methods below. It's usually advised to experiment with a couple of them, so that you can find the one that fits you best.

Disclaimer: you don't have to practice Divination to be a "good" witch or Pagan. If the thought makes you uncomfortable or afraid, please listen to yourself. It means you're not ready yet. And if that's the case, please feel free to skip this chapter and go straight to the chapter about seasonal spells. But if uncovering the secrets of the future thrills you even just a little bit… then please, keep reading!

FIND THE PRACTICE THAT SUITS YOU

In this day and age, a Witch is spoiled for choice when it comes to divination practices.

Some of us practice only one method that we feel "speaks" to us more, others like to combine different methods or try different things depending on our mood and the seasons.

Let's go through the most common divination methods together, shall we?

Astrology

The art of looking at the position and movement of the stars in the sky to make predictions about the future has been around since the ancient Babylonians — and became especially popular in Ptolemaic Egypt through the Hermetic texts (as we've seen on the first part of this book, when we discussed the origins of secret organizations like Golden Dawn). It's true that since the revival of Pagan practices after the 19th century, astrology has become both extremely popular and mainstream, but at the same time it's also considered a "less than" spiritual practice. Perhaps it's all these astrology hotlines out there?

Regardless, the art of astrology is not for the faint of heart. Truly understanding the movements of the planets, how they interact with one another and how this interaction can affect one's natal chart and future is an intricate process — not recommended if you're just starting on your path and need some answers fast! (Please, don't call a hotline.)

On the other hand, because astrology is such an intricate technique, as long as you do the calculations and you consult the charts and timetables, there is usually not a big margin for error — or variations in personal interpretation. So you can feel more "secure" in your predictions.

Cheiromancy

Also known as palmistry, the art of reading one's palm to ascertain the future has been practiced all over the world — and every culture has its own explanations for what every line, peak and valley of your palm really means. Very popular among Roma fortune tellers, palmistry to this day also has a "parlor trick" flair among modern witches and sceptics alike.

Palmistry is easier to learn than astrology, as there is a finite number of lines and features in one's hand and identifying their meanings is relatively simpler. The only "problem" with palmistry is the fact that the features of one's hand doesn't really change that much over time. So although it may be a potent tool for one-time readings, if you rely on it frequently it may give you a sense that everything is predetermined and that there's no room for growth.

And who wants to feel like that?

Cleromancy

One of the most diverse techniques out there. People throughout the ages have casted anything from lots, dice, coins, runes (as in Old Norse Pagan traditions), yarrow sticks (as in the Chinese I-Ching tradition), oil palm kernels (as in the Ifá tradition of the Yoruba) and even marbles.

Although the Ifá tradition is usually practiced by people who share the Yoruba heritage, the I-Ching is open to anyone who will take the time to study it. There are books that showcase the meanings of each throw (there are 64 hexagrams that you can create by throwing either yarrow sticks or coins) in detail[27]. Like astrology, once you understand the process there is not much room for "error" although the interpretations can be quite poetic and abstract.

---

[27] The Complete I Ching - 10th Anniversary Edition : The Definitive Translation by Taoist Master Alfred Huang, Inner Traditions Bear and Company.

Runes, basically the old Germanic/Scandinavian alphabet, has been used for both writing and divination purposes since around 150 CE. Rune divination is actually one of the best practices for witches who are just getting started! The word itself means "secret" or "hidden" and the way it works is you carve each letter of the alphabet (there are 24) in tokens — that are traditionally made of wood but can be made of stone as well. Each rune, apart from symbolizing a letter, it also symbolizes a word: for example, the rune D, Dagaz, means "day" but also "good luck" and is considered to denote spiritual growth. Note that if you order a set of runes online, one of them will be blank; this is not a mistake. The blank rune, also called "Odin's rune", symbolizes infinite potential. Talk about creating your own future!

Dowsing

A type of divination using a Y-shaped rod, traditionally used to locate water or metals. Nowadays, most people use pendants for dowsing divinations: judging by the way the chain of the pendant moves if the answer to a question is "yes" or "no". Dowsing can be an impressive divination technique, especially around ley lines and places with strong magnetic energy... but it can also be manipulated easily by the practitioner moving their hands just so.

Ouija boards

The flat boards that feature the letters of the alphabet were used as a parlor trick when first invented in 1890, but became a more "serious" divination method during World War I. Ouija boards are supposed to help you communicate easier with spirits during seances (where the spirits supposedly move the needle towards the letters they want to form words with) but like pendulum dowsing they can be easily manipulated by the person who holds the needle as well.

Prophetic dreaming

Oneiromancy is a vast field, with several books written on the subject — so we should keep it short here. In short, having prophetic dreams can be an overwhelming experience, especially if you're still new to your Path. Can you trust your prophetic dreams to come true? Especially when they're usually about bad things... And there are so many different definitions out there...

Breathe, dear one. Prophetic dreams can be a powerful tool, but only if you use them as a tool and you don't give them any dominion over your waking life. Make sure to always have a journal near your bed, so that you can write down your dreams every morning (or, since we live in 2019, use an app to take notes). Then, study their meaning later in the day, when you will have calmed down and their hold on you will have dissipated a bit. Please know that even if you dream something very bad (that's happening to you or a loved one) it doesn't mean it will take place exactly as you dreamt it. Take it more like an indication of the current energies, and work to send good vibrations and healing to the person you dreamed about.

If the dream was about you and you don't like what you saw, murmur "I give this dream no power over me" a few times, until you feel back in control of your own destiny.

Scrying

Ah, all these movies where fortune tellers look at crystal balls and see the future (or scam their clients). Scrying is an ancient and extremely difficult technique, recommended for advanced practitioners. Any reflective surface, from mirrors to crystals and water streams can be used for scrying — there is really no guidebook for scrying, as it's your intuition and the guidance you may receive from spirits and deities that will affect what you See. So please, don't spend hours looking at crystal balls, disappointed at the perceived lack of your abilities: scrying takes a lot of practice and a very specific state of mind.

A good start to get in that frame of mind, dear one, is to start meditating daily. Empty your mind, perhaps looking at the flame of a candle or a specific marking on a wall. After a while, you'll notice you're still looking at it without "really looking at it". That's the type of "soft but focused" looking you need to use when scrying. You'll get it right, eventually.

Tarot cards

Is it you, or are tarot cards EVERYWHERE lately? It's not you, dear one.

Tarot cards, also known as cartomancy, have been used for divination since around 1750 CE, in Italy and France — but soon became popular throughout Europe. Back then, the preferred decks were the Tarocco Bolognese and the Tarot of Marseilles, but the usage of tarot cards in Victorian secret societies such as the Golden Dawn (see first part of the book) increased the creation of tarot deck designs and started a competition between occultists about whose tarot deck version is considered the "best". We've already seen that Aleister Crowly created his own tarot deck, the Thoth tarot, but the Rider-Waite tarot deck (that draws inspiration from 19th century occultist Eliphas Levi) was back then and remains to this day the most commonly used tarot deck.

Tarot cards are perhaps the best way for beginners on the Path to practice divination and sharpen their intuition. Trust that your life will change once you incorporate daily tarot card readings in your schedule! Not because the Tarot cards have all the answers and will tell you what to do (definitely not, nobody has ALL the answers) but because their suggestive imagery is strong enough to guide your intuition but also soft enough to let you draw your own conclusions and hone your skills. Start by pulling one card a day — and reading the detailed guide below!

UNDERSTAND THE TAROT CARD MEANINGS

Tarot cards have changed a lot throughout the ages — nowadays there are hundreds of cool versions of tarot decks out there! You should definitely do some research to find a deck that speaks to you, but it is recommended, dear one, to start with the traditional Rider-Waite tarot deck. Once you unlock the meanings of the traditional cards, you'll be better equipped to understand modern tarot decks.

So buckle up, as we embark on a journey through the Major and Minor Arcana of the Rider-Waite tarot deck. Ready? Great!

The Major Arcana consists of 22 cards, numbered from 0 to 21. These cards depict the major events in a person's life; the stages of our journey through life. In fact, many believe that if you put all the Major Arcana cards one next to the other, they tell a story. Try it out; it will help you understand their narrative better.

But for now, let's examine the cards one by one, shall we?

Card Number: 0

Card Name: The Fool

The Fool describes new adventures — and the hubris with which we sometimes undertake them. The card shows a young man striking out on his first adventure, full of excitement for what's to come and cheered on by his loyal dog. The sun shines brightly on him: we can't help but share in the boundless optimism of this image! The ignorance and confidence we sometimes display at the beginning of a journey can be beneficial: there are some tasks so arduous we would never take them on if we knew better. He carries his belongings at the end of a wand, which symbolizes the energy, creativity and strength The Fool is bringing with him in this new journey. If successful, we will develop new skills, new perspectives and make new friends along the way... But The Fool also reminds us to be cautious, dear one. When starting a new chapter in our lives, too much confidence can be just as bad as too little. Imagine if we tripped and fell before we even began!

Card Number: 1

Card Name: The Magician

The Magician reminds us we have everything we need in order to succeed. We simply need to look around us. The card shows a highly-skilled individual who knows how to harness his full potential, straddling the space between the internal and the external realm. He extends his hands in opposite directions to remind us that, "as above, so below". (Isn't that as Pagan as it gets?) The Magician is surrounded by tools that symbolize the four elements: a sword for Air, a wand for Fire, a cup for Water and a pentacle for Earth. Holding a white wand in his one hand and pointing at the lush flowers blooming around his feet, he declares his ability to control his own Destiny. An Ouroboros around his waist and the symbol of infinity crowning him like a halo, are here to remind us of the eternal nature of The Magician's inner power — and our own. If we don't believe in own our ability to shape our life as we desire, we will never manifest our full potential. This card can also be a warning that we've been relying too much on other people and failing to take full responsibility for the lessons the Universe is serving us.

Card Number: 2

Card Name: The High Priestess

The High Priestess connects us with our feminine energy and reminds us to sit still and trust our intuition. We will realize we knew the answer to the question that's been troubling us, all along.

She is an invitation to go deeper, connect to our spiritual self and listen to the messages from our subconscious: sitting at the entrance of the Temple of Sacred Knowledge, where only the truly wise can enter. She is flanked by two columns, one black and one white, symbolizing again the Pagan duality (day and night, male and female, yin and yang). Her clothes are flowy like water and simmering like the Moon which graces her feet. The Moon is also present in the crown she is wearing, shaped after its three facets: the crescent, the Full Moon and the waning moon; the three faces of the Goddess. A cross in her chest and the scroll in her hands show that The High Priestess possess the secrets to divine knowledge but does not offer access to them freely. With this card, it is possible that we will find that secrets are being kept from us. It can also show that we've been hesitant to act.

Card Number: 3

Card Name: The Empress

The Empress symbolizes fertility and motherhood: she is exactly the Divine Feminine worshipped by our ancestors so many millennia ago... The card is showing her nesting amid a lush forest, sitting on a throne of comfortable red cushions, adorned with the symbol of Venus. A crown of twelve stars graces her blond hair and her long robe is embellished with pomegranates, for fertility and abundance. The river of Life is flowing near The Empress' feet and she stands as beautiful and benevolent as the trees surrounding her. Now is a great time to give birth to new creative projects and see them blossom and grow. We should express our affections and nurture the creatures surrounding us, be they humans, animals or plants — but not overdo it. Too much water can kill a plant, as too much affection can spoil or suffocate a person. Are we over-infantilizing someone, believing they need us more than they actually do?

Card Number: 4

Card Name: The Emperor

The Emperor is calling us to be as confident in our strength as he is. He rules bravely, with fierce determination. The card shows him at the feet of a craggy mountain, sitting on his austere throne — the only embellishment being the four heads of rams, symbolizing his success in battle and his association with Aries. The Emperor is, after all, a warrior King: he may be holding they symbols of the world of the living he is ruling (the Orb and the Ankh), but he wears the full body armor of a Knight underneath his red cloak. We are called to ascertain our dominion over a situation, or to protect those dear to us, never failing to establish order where we need to. Although, like every stern ruler, we may not always be beloved when we find ourselves in positions of power. Are we holding the reins too tight?

Card Number: 5

Card Name: The Hierophant

The Hierophant is the ultimate teacher; the mentor figure we need to guide us through moral dilemmas, the education institution who can help us unlock our potential for knowledge and understanding. Like The High Priestess, The Hierophant is also sitting at the entrance of a Temple, flanked by two marble columns. But his realm of knowledge is not just the subconscious: he equally rules the conscious, subconscious and superconscious, something made apparent by his three crowns, three papal robes and the three-cross scepter he is holding. The Hierophant is presiding over the traditions and customs that allow our society to function, the keys to the kingdom of men on his feet. Kneeling before him are two of his acolytes, their heads traditionally shaved in the style of Capuchin monks, symbolising piety. We can emulate the values of The Hierophant and assume a mentoring role towards others, sharing our hard-earned wisdom. But we should be careful to not be blinded by our own beliefs or becoming too attached to our own habits. "Different" doesn't always have to mean "a threat".

Card Number: 6

Card Name: The Lovers

The Lovers represent the divine pairing, the balanced union of perfect opposites. In this card, The Lovers stand completely naked, facing each other as equals. They're in the Garden of Eden: behind the woman, the Tree of Knowledge is ripe with fruit but the Serpent, symbolizing temptation is circling it. Behind the man, a tree made of flames represents his fiery passion. The Lovers are blessed and protected by the Archangel Raphael, who is sending them a gust of wind to facilitate communication. A radiant Sun, symbolizing happiness, shines on them both. In our own lives, The Lovers symbolize all these relationships, be they romantic, platonic or even professional, that complete us and bring harmony into our lives. But this card is also a warning not to linger too long in indecision, or stay in relationships that no longer serve our growth.

Card Number: 7

*Card Name: **The Chariot***

The Chariot reminds us to be in the driver's seat of our life, reigning in any external hindrances and charting a clear course towards our goals. Like the warrior in this card, who stands ready for action. He has no horses to reign in: at the feet of The Chariot, a black and a white sphinx, symbolizing opposite forces, are resting. But the warrior will move The Chariot through the power of his will, represented by his white wand. Cosmic symbols, from the Sun on his head to the Moon on his shoulders, assure of his success and remind us we don't have to rely on excessive strength to triumph. We just need to keep our eyes focused on where we want to go and we will surpass any obstacles along the way. As long as we don't forget our true path in life!

Card Number: 8

*Card Name: **Strength***

The message of the Strength card is not to stifle our basic instincts or ignore our desires. Like the woman with her hands on the lion's mouth depicted on this card, we too need to lovingly acknowledge our raw emotions (the lion) and then rise above them. With her hands wrapped gently around the open mouth of a fierce lion, the woman proves that Strength is much more than mere physical might. Her long white dress, adorned with flowers, speak to the purity of her intentions and her inner beauty. The symbol of infinity over her head shows her endless potential. Showing compassion, both to ourselves and to others who need our help, is what true Strength means. But we shouldn't become too confident in our own abilities, or care more about how people perceive us than about how we can use our gifts to help them... That's not strength, dear one, that's pride.

Card Number: 9

Card Name: The Hermit

The Hermit asks us to take a step back from our busy schedules, in order to see the bigger picture. Perhaps we have been focusing too much on being surrounded by other people and material comforts, and we have forgotten who we truly are at the core of our being. In the card, The Hermit stands alone on the summit of a snowy mountain, his only source of light being the Six-Pointed Star inside his lantern, a symbol of wisdom. Covered in simple gray robes, The Hermit may be old but he possesses knowledge and authority, represented by his long wooden staff which supports him as he carefully makes his next steps. Spending some time alone, reading or meditating, may be all we need in order to return to the outside world all the wiser for it. But we shouldn't withdraw too much into our own shell. No one is happy being alone forever.

Card Number: 10

Card Name: Wheel of Fortune

A harbinger of good news and serendipity, the Wheel of Fortune is here to remind us that no matter how trapped we may be feeling in our current situation, change is always just around the corner. The Wheel of Fortune, adorned with the alchemical symbols for the four elements and surrounded by a serpent (for evil), Anubis (for the dead and the living) and a Sphinx (for wisdom), represents the circle of life. Just like life, The Wheel of Fortune contains both the good and the bad, forever spinning in mid-air. At the four corners of the sky, winged creatures symbolising the fixed signs in astrology (Aquarius, Scorpio, Taurus and Leo) illustrate our ability to find stillness and control even amid frantic change. We shouldn't hesitate to embrace that change: the Wheel of Fortune favors the bold. But we should also remember that goes around comes around. Have we been attracting good karma into our lives?

Card Number: 11

Card Name: Justice

As the Wheel of Fortune brings us karma, so does Justice make sure that our actions have the consequences they deserve. Seated between two grey pillars, holding the scales on one hand and an upright sword in the other, Justice is the manifestation of law. Cloaked in regal red, with a squared crown representing rational thought and her white shoes declaring her pureness, Justice combines logical assessment with the need to listen to one's intuition. A purple veil hanging between the two pillars, implies that Justice is here to deliver the wisdom of a Higher power. Whether we are waiting on some personal or professional assessment or we are dealing with legal matters, Justice reassures us that, if we have been truthful and virtuous, we have nothing to fear. But if we are quick to judge a person or a situation, we should ask ourselves: would we apply the same standards to us?

Card Number: 12

Card Name: The Hanged Man

The Hanged Man asks us to let go of what we previously thought possible, or inevitable. Hanging by his right foot, The Hanged Man has chosen this fate on his own volition: as his free left foot shows, he can disentangle himself at any time. The Hanged Man seeks clarity and is willing to suspend himself from the Tree of Life in order to gain a different perspective. His red pants and blue shirt symbolize a balance between his passions and his controlled emotions, whereas his yellow shoes and his vibrant halo are symbols of his brilliance. His state of surrender is teaching us patience and alerts us that the time is not right yet to make any big changes. If we "hang in there" a little bit more, answers will surely come. But let's be honest with ourselves: do we perhaps love to play the martyr? Drawing attention to the sacrifices we've endured for the greater good?

Card Number: 13

Card Name: Death

Don't be afraid, dear one! The Death card's message is kind and necessary: we shouldn't resist change. As the sun sets Death rides on his white horse, his banner of a five-pointed flower representing change. A skeleton in a black armor, Death is at the same time inevitable and indestructible: no one can escape the change he brings, although many (from a bishop to a child) will try. In the river behind him, a black boat is heading towards the Towers of the setting sun, already carrying the soul of the fallen king who sleeps peacefully and eternally underneath Death's horse. Knowing that transformation is one of the most important aspects of life, Death wants us to embrace the closing of a certain chapter. It's the only way for us to start a new, better one. As long as we don't hold on to grief more than we really have to...

Card Number: 14

Card Name: Temperance

Temperance is a reminder for the need of diplomacy: we need to listen to both sides of the argument and to put strong feelings aside in order to overcome our differences. With one foot firmly on the ground and the other dipped in the water, the angel of Temperance is here to balance the elements and bring harmony. Simultaneously feminine, masculine and genderless, Temperance is delicately pouring water from one golden cup to another, representing the eternal flow between the conscious and subconscious mind, but also the need to temper our emotions. At the end of the road behind the angel the Sun burns bright, as Temperance paves the way to Enlightenment. It's by being equally open to other people's feedback and our own intuition, that we will manage to achieve harmony. As long as we don't use diplomacy as a way to avoid taking a stand.

Card Number: 15

Card Name: The Devil

The Devil is a warning that our worst instincts (jealousy, cruelty, greed, insatiability) may be getting the best of us, trapping us in a prison of our own making. Once free and comfortable in their nakedness, the lovers are now chained at the feet of The Devil. With the torso of a man, the feet of a goat and the wings of a bat (we should remember here that the Pagan symbols in this deck are sometimes used through a Christian lens), The Devil is a representation of what happens when our more animalistic side takes over. Looming over his victims on a pedestal, The Devil raises one hand in salutation while setting fire to the man with the other. Although he seems to have complete control over the lovers, their chains are loose and their hands are free: they could choose to liberate themselves at any time. Just like the lovers who are loosely chained however, we too can break free from our bad habits if we decide to. We don't have to completely surrender our sense of self-control just to have some fun. The Devil invites us to savor everything life has to offer, but the task of determining the cost is up to us.

Card Number: 16

Card Name: The Tower

The Tower requires us to embrace the change. When lighting strikes The Tower in this card, everything will be illuminated; no secrets will remain hidden. This sudden upheaval is happening so that we can be freed from any structures, relationships and bonds that do not serve us anymore, even if we were oblivious to their problems until now. The Tower appears to be a solid construction at first glance — but if we look at its base, it becomes clear that it was built upon uneven and shaky foundations. Amid the chaos wrought by the lighting, two people are falling from The Tower's windows in desperation. Surrounding them, 22 flames lit up the sky (for the 22 steps in the Major Arcana journey), symbolizing that this upheaval is too part of life and cannot be avoided. We need to jump from the crumbling structure in order to be saved, not freeze in panic or try to pretend this is not happening.

Card Number: 17

Card Name: The Star

The Star is here to light our way and guide us towards a better day.Just as the angel of Temperance had one foot on the ground and the other immersed in water, so does this naked woman, kneeling gracefully under the light of The Star. But while

Temperance poured water from one cup to the other, in The Star the woman is opening the circuit; using two clay urns, she is taking water from the pond with her right hand and watering the earth with her left. Behind her, a bird perched upon a lush tree represents inspiration. Above her, seven smaller stars symbolize the seven chakras of the human body. An indication that the odds are in our favor, The Star urges us to start dreaming big once again and having hope that our dreams will be fulfilled. We should never be too jaded to believe in happy endings!

Card Number: 18

Card Name: The Moon

The Moon is here to guide us when not everything is as it seems. We can find our way through any uncertainty, as long as we accept the limitations of our rational mind and trust our intuition and subconscious. Ruler of the realm of mysteries, The Moon shines its light on the creatures of the night, bringing forth dualities in all things: the twin towers of Good and Evil are indistinguishable from one another; the tame dog is barking at The Moon like his wild brother, the wolf. Amid this dreamy landscape a crawfish steps slowly out of the waters to follow the path towards the unknown, beyond the towers and the mountains in the distance. Just like in dream logic, believing in things we may not entirely understand may be our safest way forward. We will need to embrace this period of uncertainty and not let our fears and anxieties get the best of us.

Card Number: 19

Card Name: The Sun

As his light helps the crops grow strong, so does The Sun's influence in our life brings us all our heart's desire. The dark night of The Moon is now but a distant memory: It's a new day and a brand new start. Four sunflowers, representing the four suits of the Minor Arcana, emerge from behind a gray wall whereas in front of it, a small naked child is riding a white horse, symbolizing innocence, vitality and nobility. The child waves a banner in the color of blood, representing renewal, new life and happiness. Health, prosperity and success in our endeavors; a happy family and home; new creative projects that will bring us the recognition we've been craving: nothing is impossible under the nurturing light of The Sun. We should be grateful for all our blessings, dear one.

Card Number: 20

Card Name: Judgement

Judgement comes to remind us to take stock of our actions and recognize our failings. As the Archangel Gabriel blows his trumpet, the dead are rising from their graves: men, women and children, naked and smiling, all extend their hands towards the Archangel in bliss. Hanging from the Judgement's trumpet, a square white flag with a red cross represents the four stages of life and the sacrifices needed in order to achieve purity and rebirth. There is still time to atone for any mistakes; to see our efforts rewarded and a conflict concluding favorably. Judgement, ultimately, represents forgiveness: forgiveness we need to extend toward others, but also to ourselves. Judgement will not be in our favor if we are not truly humble.

Card Number: 21

Card Name: The World

The World signifies our achievements, when we have come full circle and can reap our rewards. As the angel, the eagle, the lion and the bull (the four representations of the fixed signs of the zodiac) stood at the four corners of the Wheel of Fortune, so they stand now at the four corners of The World. A dancing woman, naked but for a purple cloth that represents wisdom, is constantly spinning within a circle of laurels, symbolizing evolution and success. Holding two white wands similar to the one The Magician held, the woman is bringing the magic full circle: everything has manifested as it was supposed to. We are content and complete, at peace with the people and the situations surrounding us. This perfect harmony is a time to rest and just be happy, before we start planning our next adventure. Can we pack it all up and try again?

Now that you've mastered the Major Arcana, it's time to dive into the Minor Arcana.

The Minor Arcana consists of 4 suits: Pentacles, Swords, Wands and Cups. Yes, dear one, they look a bit similar to the playing cards: there are number cards from Ace to Ten and then Pages, Knights, Queens and Kings for each suit. Only here the goal is not to collect as many Kings or Aces as possible as you do in poker. It's to understand the significance of this, the more "mundane" part of the tarot cards that speaks to everyday situations.

Ready to start?

Pentacles

The Pentacles suit is associated with Winter (that's why it's usually mentioned first) and with the element of Earth. Cards of this suit speak mostly about "earthly" matters such as money, material security, work, matters of the home, generosity and materialism.

Ace of Pentacles

Emerging from a cloud amid a grey sky, an aetherial hand surrounded by a halo is holding the Ace of Pentacles like a generous offering. The coin, its bright yellow color representing both material treasures (gold) and divine knowledge, contains an engraved pentacle: all four elements of life on Earth, bound together by Spirit. Underneath the divine offering, we see a garden with blooming white lilies — a symbol of innocence and purity, but also of abundance. A gate made from rose bushes, representing morality leads a yellow path toward the mountains in the distance and the higher knowledge that awaits there.

The Ace of Pentacles, like all Aces in the Minor Arcana, signals a new beginning. The Pentacles being the suit of Earth, this new beginning will most likely involve our career or our finances. It's a great time to make investments or start a new job, but this card is also a good sign when it comes to health issues or moving to a new home.

But the Ace of Pentacles can also imply a materialistic streak in our personality and a tendency to play it safe. Do we care about money a little too much?

Two of Pentacles

A young man wearing a very tall red hat, representing a passionate connection between his own thoughts and the divine inspiration that comes from the sky, is balancing the Two of Pentacles in his hands. Standing on one leg, the man holds the two coins intertwined in a green cloth, shaped like the infinity symbol: his balancing act is both rooted in the present and adaptable to chances, but also of a timeless quality. Behind him, the sea seems quite turbulent, with two ships performing their own balancing act, riding the waves high. It is a symbol of the man's turbulent thoughts and subconscious, but the fact that he is actually standing on firm ground, wearing green shoes, means that he is currently thriving despite the challenges.

Like the man in the Two of Pentacles card, we too are currently thriving — although it probably takes a lot of multitasking. Whether it's working two jobs and having two sources of income or simply weighing our options and budgeting wisely between our needs and wants, the Two of Pentacles is a sign that we are currently in perfect balance.

The Two of Pentacles however is a volatile card: the tables can be overturned very easily, leaving us feeling overwhelmed. Have we taken on more responsibilities than we can handle?

Three of Pentacles

A young man is working as an apprentice stonemason at a cathedral, where the Three of Pentacles are carved in the stone. He momentarily stops working to acknowledge the two people beside him: a priest and a nobleman dressed in a colorful outfit. They are holding the plans for the design of the cathedral and they seem eager to discuss them with the stonemason. Despite his more modest clothes implying a lesser social status than the other two men, the stonemason is standing on a bench and is being looked up to, indicating that although they all come from different walks of life, this construction is a teamwork where practical skills are necessary and held in high esteem.

The Three of Pentacles means that we will need to work with a team in order to achieve our goals — we shouldn't hesitate consulting people who come from a different background than ours. The Three of Pentacles is also a sign that we are honing our skills and getting valuable experience. We are on our way to greatness.

But the Three of Pentacles can also mean we are relying too much on what other people think about us, or about our work. Would it be better to shut down the outside noise and just focus on our work?

Four of Pentacles

A man, sitting on a stone bench overlooking a city, has a firm grip on the Four of Pentacles. One of the coins is balancing on his head, over his golden crown, while the others are stomped underneath his feet and held close to his chest, representing an unwillingness to part with wealth or material comforts. His black fur coat over his red cloak is keeping him warm, but it is also a symbol of how his wealth has isolated the man from all the people in the city behind him. The position of the man's hands around one of the coins resemble Ouroboros (the snake that feeds on itself), further indicating a closed system with no space for outside influences.

The Four of Pentacles is certainly a positive card for our bank account. It denotes financial stability and material comforts, a luxurious home where we are being surrounded by beautiful things. The card also speaks to our ability to save money, often to a great social cost, like avoiding going out with friends in order to not overspend.

But the Four of Pentacles is also a great warning that we have become too greedy and stingy with money. Are we losing our inner joy just to add a few more coins into our savings?

Five of Pentacles

During a snowy night two raggedy beggars are passing outside a church, the Five of Pentacles gleaming with light from its stained glass window. The beggars are scarcely clothed, partially barefoot and one of them is using clutches, a representation of the many adversities a person can face in life. The church window has a warm glow and its decoration with leaves, flowers, and a candelabra holding the Five of Pentacles, symbolizes the possibility of safety and abundance that is currently being denied to the two poor passers by. It is also possible however that the beggars are so preoccupied with their own struggles, they don't notice that salvation is within reach.

The polar opposite of Four of Pentacles, Five of Pentacles warns us about hard times and financial adversity. Perhaps we will be faced with unexpected fees to pay, or spent a period of austerity to compensate for previous overspending. Although a worrisome card, the Five of Pentacles is mostly here to remind us that hope and help are always within reach, we just need to know where to look.

But the Five of Pentacles can also be a warning of a more dangerous kind of poverty: the emotional one. Have we been isolating ourselves from the beloved people in our lives, those who are our true source of wealth?

Six of Pentacles

Almost like in a continuation of the story depicted in Five of Pentacles, here the two poor beggars seem to have found mercy and charity under the protection of the Six of Pentacles. Wrapped in warm cloaks, they are kneeling in front of a man who is handing them out coins with his right hand while holding a scale with his left — suggesting an evening out of resources and, perhaps, karma. The scale is almost in balance but not fully, hinting that it is better to always err a bit more on the side of giving. The city with its high rising towers in the background brings to mind the rich ruler of Four of Pentacles, only this time the wealthy man has left the isolation of his rich and secure home to help out the less fortunate.

Whether we identify more with the giving or the receiving aspect of Six of Pentacles, this card is here to remind us that both are necessary in life. We shouldn't be too proud to ask for help, or too cold hearted to help others. It doesn't have to be about money even: charity takes many forms.

The Six of Pentacles however can be a perfect example of how good intentions, sometimes have bad results. Is constantly giving to someone making them too dependent on us?

Seven of Pentacles

After raking leaves for what seems to be really long time, a man is currently resting on his rake, admiring the pile of leaves that is blossoming with the Seven of Pentacles. He looks slightly despondent and tired, as if he can do nothing more at this point but wait, although upon closer inspection we can see there is more work to be done -- and more to be gained by doing it. The man is wearing two different colored shoes, a symbol of being halfway there.

The Seven of Pentacles represents that lack of energy we feel toward the end of the working week, when the reward of the weekend is within sight, but not there yet. In a broader sense, Seven of Pentacles represents the need for patience. We have been working hard and perhaps we haven't yet seen the result we would like. But the best is yet to come if we just keep going.

The Seven of Pentacles also warns of our tendency to be distracted, when a task becomes repetitive and boring. Is it taking us longer to finish our work because our head is not in the game?

Eight of Pentacles

A man wearing a work apron and straddling a bench, an allegory for him being "on top" of the situation, labors hard with etching the coins in Eight of Pentacles. He is very present, focused and diligent in his craft and he has already finished a stack of pentacles who are now attached to a tree, suggesting growth. His red trousers and shoes represent his passion and determination, while his blue shirt shows he is calm and serene in his work. A town is visible further away, a further representation that, unlike his Seven of Pentacles counterpart, this man has left all distractions far behind.

The Eight of Pentacles is a sign we are in the "zone", taking pleasure in our work and in the reputation we are building for ourselves. Apart from actual work matters (a possible promotion that comes with its share of extra responsibilities and a raise), this card may also represent our ability to think practically, use the tools that we have in any given situation and ultimately excel at anything.

But the Eight of Pentacles also warns us about the dangers of workaholism. Have we become too enveloped in our work that we've forgotten to have a life?

Nine of Pentacles

A lavishly dressed woman enjoys the bounty of her vineyard, surrounded by the Nine of Pentacles. She holds a hooded falcon in her left hand, a symbol of her intellectual superiority but also of her self control. The gold and red colors of her clothes represent an enviable financial and social standing, whereas her light touching of the grapes and the coin suggest that the woman is not too concerned about money. Further financial stability is implied by the large house at the back whereas in front of her, on the ground, a small snail signifies that this luxurious life took her a while, but her patience has finally been rewarded.

Like the woman in the NIne of Pentacles, so are we able to create our own safe space, exactly as we want it. Whether it's an actual home, an unconventional relationship or an allegory for our own state of mind, the Nine of Pentacles is here to remind us that we already have everything we need in order to be happy.

The NIne of Pentacles however can also represent a tendency to show-off. Are we living beyond our means simply to impress other people?

Ten of Pentacles

An old man is sitting in the company of two dotting dogs, a couple and a child just further away: it's a family gathering, accentuated by the Ten of Pentacles. The old man's vividly decorated robe suggests his many accomplishments, with patterns of vines and grapes speaking of a luxurious lifestyle. He is petting one of the dogs while the child is petting the other, indicating a family that is bonded together by trust and loyalty. They all seem to be inside a castle's walls, a symbol of prosperity at home and financial security.

Like all the cards with the number ten in the Minor Arcana, the Ten of Pentacles represents the culmination of our efforts; our hard work being rewarded. Whether it is a much wanted promotion or a source of income that will really make a difference in our lives, the Ten of Pentacles speaks of abundance and prosperity. If we are considering moving to a bigger house, this card is a very positive sign that we should.

The Ten of Pentacles, although an inherently positive card, can also be a sign that we are using our newfound wealth (or our family's wealth) in an immoral way. Are we trying to buy ourselves special treatment?

Page of Pentacles

Standing on a green and luscious hill, the Page of Pentacles is admiring his fortune. Dressed in brown and green, to signify stability and prosperity, the page has nonetheless a vibrant red hat on, a sign that he is passionate and proud of his new achievement. A small grove of trees to the left and a plot of freshly plowed land on the right signify a fertile ground for new developments and a good potential for success. There may be difficulties ahead, implied by the mountain range lining the horizon, but for now the Page of Pentacles is in a good place.

Like the Page of Pentacles, so will we achieve the most when we combine ambition with diligence. Whether it's making plans for the future, studying hard or choosing to help and support a friend, the Page of Pentacles reminds us that good things will come as long as we stay loyal, grounded and kind. We don't have to rush progress.

The Page of Pentacles however can also be a warning of sometimes being too timid for our own good. Are we not being as supportive and proud of ourselves as we are toward others?

Knight of Pentacles

The Knight of Pentacles is sitting on his black steed, a golden pentacle in his right hand. He's positioned on a hill overlooking his surroundings, a newly plowed land spreadings out at the foot of the hill. The Knight of Pentacles looks determined and calm, as if carefully considering his next steps. While the other knights of the Minor Arcana have plumes and wings on their helmet, this knight has green leaves, suggesting that his ambition is to preserve and protect what he already has, rather than go hunting for more.

The Knight of Pentacles is the perfect embodiment of the phrase "slow and steady wins the race". By being efficient and reliable, we will achieve better results than if we'd stormed into a situation without thinking things through. There's nothing wrong with having a routine.

The Knight of Pentacles however can also exasperate people with his seemingly slow pace and lack of apparent progress. Being a creature of habit is one thing, but are we being too stuck in how we're used to doing things that we don't see there is a better and faster way?

Queen of Pentacles

The Queen of Pentacles sits on her ornate throne, amid a lush forest. Her throne is carved with patterns of cherubs, ram's heads and fruit, symbols for fertility, abundance and love. Rose bushes are hanging over her and flowers abound by her feet, further depicting this queen's affinity for abundance and her love for things that bring joy to the senses. A red rabbit near her feet is a sign of her maternal and protective nature. The combination of red, green and white in her dress, along with the blue mountains and the yellow sky, symbolize that the Queen of Pentacles is the sum of many different qualities, a complex character who can best be understood as mother who will do anything to provide a safe and comfortable home for her children.

The Queen of Pentacles may represent our relationship with our mother, or some other female figure in our lives who always supports and nourishes us. This card also speaks to the supportive and nourishing aspects in ourselves and our ability to "turn a house into a home". It's overall a positive card, especially with regards to practical and domestic issues.

But like any overly doting mother, sometimes the Queen of Pentacles can be overbearing. Are we smothering our loved ones in our certainty that we know what's best for them?

King of Pentacles

Secure and proud within his castle walls, the King of Pentacles sits on an ornate throne decorated by four bulls; a symbol of steadfastness, willpower and virility. His long robe is richly decorated with vines and grapes, a depiction of success and abundance. Grapes are lying by his feet as well, scattered among luscious greens and flowers. He holds a sceptre in his right hand for cosmic power and authority, and a pentacle coin in his left for material manifestation. His left foot is resting on the head of a beast he's slain, suggesting a man of self-control.

In contrast to other Kings, the King of Pentacles can clearly appreciate the nice things in life — and he urges us to do the same. Whether he's representing a male mentor-like figure in our lives, there to help further our career, or our own steadfastness and ability to rise to the top of our field, the King of Pentacles is a very positive card. Success is here, and we should enjoy it.

But the King of Pentacles can be notorious for his inflexibility and resistance to change. Being steady and true to one's beliefs is admirable, but at what point does stubbornness become a hindrance?

Swords

The next suit is the Swords suit. Associated with Spring and with the element of Air, cards of this suit concern matters of the mind: our thoughts, worries, misconceptions, communication and ideas, the concept of truth and lies.

Ace of Swords

Emerging from a cloud amid a grey, downcast sky, an aetherial hand surrounded by a halo is brandishing the Ace of Swords. The sword is double-edged, a symbol of sharp wit and honesty, while a golden crown seemingly floats at its tip with a laurel wreath hanging from each side — all symbols of success, clarity of thought and divine inspiration. Three flames can be seen on each side of the sword, representing an equal distribution of knowledge but also a warning: truth will not always be easy, or pleasant.

The Ace of Swords is that "aha!" moment we have when everything suddenly fits together and makes sense. It can be a sudden revelation of something that was kept hidden from us: a shock at first, but we will become stronger and more successful for knowing the truth. This card also signifies a new, successful idea or project, as well as good developments in health related matters.

But like any double-edged weapon, the Ace of Swords can hurt both ourselves and those we point it against. Is honesty always the best policy? Or is sometimes saying nothing simply the most decent thing to do?

Two of Swords

With her back at the sea on a moonlit night, a blindfolded woman is seated at a stone bench. Her hands, folded in front of her chest, are brandishing two very long swords, each one pointing at a different direction. There are clearly two paths that the woman could take, but her blindfold forbids her to look at either. In the water behind her, two small and craggy islets symbolize possible obstacles, whereas The Moon above acts both as an advice to listen to our intuition and a warning to not be fooled by illusions.

Two of Swords is a card that denotes our inability to make up our minds and move forward. The choices are there, and one of them is the right one for us — but to find it we need to spend some time gathering more information and not blindly jump to conclusions.

But like the woman in the Two of Swords card, we may also be responsible for our own lack of clarity. Are we too afraid to face the truth and make a hard choice, that we spend too much time in needless deliberation?

Three of Swords

Dark, grey clouds have gathered in the sky; a heavy rain is falling. The grim weather, a metaphor for the sorrow and grief that are to come, is contrasted by a bright red heart, pierced with the Three of

Swords. The three wounds inflicted by the swords may represent the betrayal of a loved one, or heartbreak from the loss of a person or a relationship that was dear to us.

Although the Three of Swords is certainly not an auspicious card, its most valuable lesson is that our current pain and heartbreak can be used as a compass. They can point us, if not to where we need to be, at least to where we need to be away from. Because the message of the Three of Swords is very clear: we cannot carry on as we were, pretending we are fine.

But the Three of Swords can also indicate a love triangle that we are unable (and unwilling) to give up. Can our heart sustain two loves at once — and at what cost?

Four of Swords

Amid the calmness of a sanctuary, a knight lies eternally inside his tomb. On the wall above him, three swords are hanging vertically, a representation of the wounds he's suffered in the past. A fourth sword, placed under his tomb, signifies that his struggles have now ended: the knight's spirit is finally resting peacefully, something we can also gather from the position of his hands, as if he was in prayer. A stained glass window at the left part of the wall shows a depiction of a woman and a child in bright, warm colors, as if welcoming the fallen soldier back home in a loving embrace.

Four of Swords is all about the stillness that comes after the storm the Three of Swords wrought in our heart. Unlike the knight in the card though, we don't need to rest eternally. Whether we are talking about a literal nap amid a stressful working day, planning a vacation or simply taking a step back and trying to find inner calmness, thanks to the Four of Swords we will feel a sense of renewal when it's time to get back to the world again.

But the Four of Swords can also be a sign that we tend to take too many "breaks" from reality. Are we keeping ourselves hidden out of fear, to avoid getting hurt again?

Five of Swords

As the grey clouds dissipate revealing a blue sky, so is the conflict that took place in Five of Swords apparently over. A red haired man is in the process of gathering the fallen swords: he currently has two resting on his left shoulder, while picking up a third with his right hand. Two more swords are scattered in the ground, perhaps belonging to the two figures that are now walking away from the battle, toward the cleansing and healing waters of the sea. The man is looking at the two soldiers, but his look is indecipherable: are they his recuperating allies, or his vanquished enemies?

Five of Swords is a reminder that we always lose something in every conflict we choose to participate in — even when we have seemingly won. There is no honor to be found in needless fighting. Even if we believe we were on the right side of an argument, we should always remember to pick our battles.

But Five of Swords also represents our tendency to make ourselves miserable by getting hang up in past annoyances. Are we still behaving like a victim, lamenting something that's over and done with?

Six of Swords

A boat is being rowed in the calm waters, toward a peaceful-looking land. Riding on the boat is a woman completely covered in a yellow cloak, a symbol of the knowledge and wisdom that she has acquired through the many adversities she has faced. Next to her, a small child, depicts the innocence that is not yet destroyed. The Six of Swords are surrounding her, three in each side, acting both as a shield and a memory of the losses the woman and her child may have suffered.

As the boatman of Six of Swords is slowly and safely taking the family of refugees to a better place, so do we, slowly but surely, start to distance ourselves from a bad person or situation. Whether this takes the form of an actual trip, a bigger move to another place to live or simply an internal disentanglement from what has caused us harm, Six of Swords is definitely a welcome sight.

Although Six of Swords is a very gentle and positive card though, we should be careful not to confuse "moving forward" with "running away from problems". Have we left behind unresolved issues that are bound to catch up with us soon?

Seven of Swords

A man is seen leaving the military camp in a rush, a poignant red fez and shoes contradicting his otherwise humble clothing and betraying his fickle nature. He is carrying all the stolen swords he can manage (five of them are in his arms, but he has left two behind) obviously thinking he's gotten away with it himself. Unfortunately for the thief, a group of soldiers further away may have spotted him. The dark cloud gathering behind them warns that this theft will have heavier repercussions than the thief expected.

Seven of Swords is the card of secrets and deception — and of the small details that can "give us away" right when we thought we had managed to avoid getting caught red handed. Whether we are the ones doing the deceiving, or the ones being deceived, this card is always a warning to pay more attention around us and not take anything and anyone for granted.

The Seven of Swords can also signify a general lack of trust that has resulted from our less-than-ideal behavior. How can we demand the trust of others when we are not entirely trustworthy ourselves?

Eight of Swords

A woman, bound and blindfolded, is cautiously treading treacherous and slippery ground surrounded by Eight of Swords. She is using only her feet to feel her way forward; a slow, frustrating and impossible task. Behind her, placed on top of steep cliffs and overlooking the landscape, is a castle representing the days of comfort and security, now long gone. Yet the woman, much like the woman in Two of Swords, could simply choose to remove her bondage (which is nothing but a loose fabric) and free herself. It is clear that what's stopping her are not her external limitations, but her own limiting thoughts.

When the Eight of Swords appears, we need to arm ourselves with patience and, like the woman in the card, carefully put one foot in front of the other. Whether it's a relationship, a job or a financial situation that has us feeling powerless, the Eight of Sword reminds us that we can make it through — the only thing keeping us back is our own fear.

But the Eight of Swords can also represent the part of ourselves that wants to completely give in to a situation or a person, despite knowing it will probably cost us. Are we surrendering the control of our life to someone undeserving?

Nine of Swords

A person is sitting up in bed in the middle of the night, unable to sleep. We can't tell if it is a man or a woman, as they cover their face in their hands in desperation, a sign that they have lost themselves in despair — they can no longer stand to even look at the situation they find themselves in. Nine swords are hovering against the black backdrop, representing all the threatening thoughts looming over that person's psyche. The mattress of the carved, wooden bed is thin, providing little comfort, while the duvet is a patchwork of symbols: thorny roses and astrological signs, symbolic of the forces of destiny and the struggles of everyday life.

Nine of Swords is perhaps one of the least comforting cards; an embodiment of our worst fears. However, this card is here to remind us that these dark thoughts that keep us up at night are nothing more than that: just dark thoughts. Maybe right now we are feeling vulnerable and insecure, but these feelings will melt away the next day, when the sun comes up.

Nine of Swords is also a reminder not to face our demons on our own. When we are going through an existential dark night of the soul, isn't there someone we could call for help?

Ten of Swords

A man is lying face down in the mud, stabbed with the Ten of Swords. His red cape reminiscent of a bloodbath, represents his past victories which could not save him this time, while his yellowish hand is eerily twisted and lifeless. As to punctuate the sense of ending, the sun is yielding in the horizon, drowning in a heavy blanket of pitch-black sky. The mountains and the ocean however have a soothing blue color and the waters are still. There is silence and peace, at last.

Like all the suit cards with the number 10, the Ten of Swords indicates a finale, a curtain call. And despite the fact that this finale does not seem to be a very pleasant one, neither for the protagonist nor for us, we can find comfort in the fact that we have hit rock bottom. From now on, there's nowhere to go but up.

But the Ten of Swords can also signify our flair for melodrama. Have we really been stabbed in the back by others, or do we like to pretend so to excuse our own shortcomings?

Page of Swords

The clouds may be gathering in the sky and the wind blowing like crazy, but the Page of Swords is ready — his stance reminiscent of a baseball batter ready to strike. His thick hair, a symbol of youthfulness and vitality, is waving like a flag as the winds are gathering in strength. He may be on foot, but he is also unburdened by heavy armor, his simple robes allowing him to move swiftly and adapt. For now he has the high ground, standing on the green grass.

The Page of Swords is a great communicator, always bringing new ideas to the table. This card encourages us to speak openly and passionately about the things or the people who have sparked our interest. We may not be entirely sure yet how to bring our new exciting project to completion, or how to take the next step with that fascinating person, but our intention is set. And that makes all the difference.

The Page of Swords aptitude for communication however also makes him a talented liar. When we know that with very little effort, we can present a version of the events that serves our needs better, what's keeping us honest?

Knight of Swords

The sight of trees bending from the wind and the sharp edges of the clouds herald the coming of a storm. Unfazed, maybe even excited, the Knight of Swords is charging ahead with his sword raised — forward and upward, signifying progress and expansion. The plume of his helmet and the fiery mane of his noble steed are animated both by the winds of storm and the winds of the speed with which the Knight of Sword charges forward. The horse's saddle is decorated with flying creatures: butterflies and birds, representing speed, quick wit and freedom of thought.

The Knight of Swords is an unstoppable force that wants to take us along for the ride: when this card appears, there is no room for hesitating or seconguessing ourselves. Whether we want to grab the attention of a potential new love interest or achieve a professional milestone, the Knight of Swords is giving us the horsepower to hit our goal, fast. Where there is a will, there is a way.

But as the Knight of Swords does not seem to care about the well being of his horse while he marches on as fast as possible, so do we sometimes become insensitive to others in our hurry to get things done.

Queen of Swords

As if asking her subjects to rise up to the occasion, the Queen of Swords is raising her left hand, holding a sword upright with the other. Behind her the sky is accumulating clouds but the Queen seems to be rising above them. Her rational grey robe is adorned by the blue of the sky, representing emotional stability and clear thinking. Both her crown and the carvings of her throne depict winged creatures, from cherubs to butterflies, symbols of divine inspiration and the free flow of ideas. Flying above her head, a single bird symbolizes the holy spirit, making the Queen of Sword's judgement a fair and wise one.

Like the Queen of Swords, we too are expected to exercise a fair judgement in all things and use our communication skills for good. This card also represents a woman who can be our mentor, or the smart friend who always knows how to help us make it out of a tough spot.

But the Queen of Swords can also be a warning: do we consider ourselves too smart to mingle with other people? Being haughty will only bring loneliness in the long run.

King of Swords

With his face chiseled by a stern severity, the King of Swords sits on his throne. He is holding a sword in his right hand, but the blade is slightly tilted, as if ready to bestow a knighthood rather than attack. Hir robe, blue as the heaven behind him, represents the King's absolute control over his emotions and his total clarity of thought. His cape however, glowing red on the inside, reminds us that we shouldn't be fooled by his calm exterior: this King is as powerful as the King of Wands, and will not hesitate to exert his power on others. His diadem and throne are adorned with butterflies and cherubs, symbolizing freedom of thought and divine inspiration.

The King of Swords usually represents that wise older male friend or mentor figure in our lives, who always seems to know what we should do, even when we are unsure of our own actions. But it also represents our inner voice of reason, for all those times when we need to put our head before our heart.

Like any powerful King, the King of Swords can be violent — although his weapon of choice will be words. But aren't words, when yielded with precision and bad intention, able to cut deeper than any sword?

Wands

The next suit is the Wands suit. Associated with Summer and with the element of Fire, cards of this suit speak to our fiery nature: our passion, our creativity, our sense of adventure and celebration, but also our power struggles and desires.

Ace of Wands

Emerging from a cloud, a white, aetherial hand surrounded by a halo, is holding a wooden stave: the Ace of Wands. The stave is still alive and growing: new leaves are sprouting while some leaves are being shed. The equal amount of leaves falling from each side of the wand represents a balance between the spiritual and the physical energies — and the equal opportunities that will be presented in both realms. In the distance, a castle behind some mountain peaks represents a journey that will be challenging, but worth it.

As the aetherial hand seems to be offering the Ace of Wands, so are we being offered an opportunity for renewal whenever we come across this card. Whether it is a new job opportunity, a project that will allow our creative self to flourish, or a newfound excitement about a person in our lives, the Ace of Wands is an indisputable sign to march forward.

But the Ace of Wands, although an inherently positive card, can also sometimes indicate a tendency to burn too bright, too fast. Are we too seduced by the prize (like the castle in the distance) that we underestimate the effort it will take for us to grasp it?

Two of Wands

Standing atop his castle walls surrounded by Two of Wands, a man is gazing towards the horizon. The castle, representing past successes and a reluctance to move forward, overlooks a beautiful but diverse scenery. Resting his left arm on one of the wands, the man is holding a globe in his right hand, symbolizing the infinite potential that awaits him once he ventures outside his castle walls. The man is dressed in fine robes in the colors of fire (orange and red), depicting his enviable current social status but also his zest for life.

Before embarking on our next exciting adventure, Two of Wands is here to remind us to take a pause for a moment and consider our best way forward. By taking inventory, focusing on our goals and applying careful deliberation, the success of our creative endeavors is all but assured.

But Two of Wands also warns us not to spend too much time on our comfort zone that we let an opportunity pass us by. Resting on our laurels may be comfortable, but does it also prevent us from winning more battles?

Three of Wands

Perched on the edge of a cliff, a man surrounded by Three of Wands is gazing at the sea, his red cloak depicting the victories he has achieved so far. Three ships, representing change and opportunities, are sailing in the horizon. The sky is yellow, representing knowledge, and the man is facing the sun — which is the source of all knowledge. The two wands on his right show the work he has done so far to get where he is, whereas the wand the man holds in his left hand symbolizes his plans for the future.

The Three of Wands indicates we've past the original phase of our journey or endeavor: we have ventured beyond our comfort zone (the castle in Two of Wands) and gathered valuable experience along the way. The future will bring expansion and success, as long as we are careful enough to keep planning ahead and flexible enough to change course as needed.

The Three of Wands however can also depict our tendency to "freeze" when something is not going according to schedule. When faced with delays, blockages and confusion, can we accept that all these hindrances along the way are also part of the journey?

Four of Wands

Rising high onto a golden sky, representing abundance, the Four Wands are joined together, creating a canopy of flowers. Underneath it, a couple dances in celebration, their hands holding flowers in the air. Both wearing white robes, representing purity, their cloaks are blue and red symbolizing the harmonious union of opposites. The couple stands in front of a grand castle, while more people are celebrating behind them.

Four Wands is the card of celebration — both literally and figuratively. In the literal sense, a wedding or a work party may be in our near future, where we are invited to attend and rejoice together with the people who are celebrating. But Four of Wands also represents all the things we have achieved so far, be they in our career or relationship, and the need to have rituals that honor our progress.

Four of Wands however, although a very positive card, can serve as a small warning not to be "all play and no work". Merrymaking is necessary when it is earned, but are we celebrating a bit too much, too soon?

Five of Wands

The Five of Wands are entangled in the air, brandished by five men holding them in opposite directions. The men are clearly interlocked in a conflict, all of them fighting multiple fronts at once, neither of them able to gain an advantage on the others. It is not clear, from their expressions, whether this is a friendly sparring match or an actual conflict — but their clothes, all in different colors, symbolize their dissimilar points of view.

The Five of Wands is here to remind us that a little healthy competition, at work or at any endeavor we are passionate about, can be a good thing as it motivates us to work harder. However, if we become too enamored with the conflict itself, we run the risk of forgetting what it is we were competing about in the first place.

The Five of Wands can also warn us of internal conflicts, that can make us lose our focus. Do we have so many contradicting thoughts and feelings that we've reached an inner impasse, unable to move forward toward achieving our goals? Are we being our own worst enemy?

Six of Wands

Surrounded by Six of Wands, a man is marching victorious. He wears a wreath on his head, symbolizing success, while another wreath is adorning the wand he is holding. Five more wands are raised by the crowd in celebration, as he gallops by. His horse is white, depicting purity and nobility, his green blanket symbolizing affluence and victory. The man's red cloak is a testament to his boldness and his pride in his achievement.

The Six of Wands is a very auspicious card, signifying that we have risen against the obstacles and now it's time to be rewarded for our endeavors. People will be looking up to us: we shouldn't shy away from accepting a leadership position, as we are clearly well-equipped to handle it.

But the Six of Wands can also mean that we are prone to "touting our own horn" a lot. When healthy pride in our accomplishments becomes vanity, we become blinded to the truth. In our attempt to impress the people around us, have we overplayed the importance of our own achievements?

Seven of Wands

Backed at the edge of a cliff, a man is fighting for his life. Holding a wand firmly with his both hands, he is pushing his opponents who are trying to overpower him from below, represented by the six other wands. His clothes (yellow, red and green) symbolize a combination of Fire and Earth; of passion and stability. Even though the odds seem to not be in his favor, he doesn't seem willing to accept defeat: as long as he doesn't back off, the battle is not lost.

Seven of Wands represent our inner courage and ability to "stand our ground" even when situations seem less than ideal. Staying committed to the path we have chosen and true to our convictions will get us through the adversity even if, at the moment, outside help does not seem very likely. It's always darker before the dawn.

The Seven of Wands however can also point to our infexibility and our inability to ask and accept help. Being constantly defensive will sooner or later exhaust us: not every battle can be won. Can we learn to let go when it's time to do so?

Eight of Wands

Like arrows, shot through the sky from a great distance, the Eight of Wands are on their way to land soon. Seemingly suspended in mid-air over a serene landscape, over a river which represents the flow of life, the wands are actually gathering speed by the second. Like the arrow of progress, the Eight of Wands are always pointing forward and, with no obstacles standing in their way, they will definitely land on their intended target.

The Eight of Wands, like a friendlier version of The Tower, represents change that will come suddenly into our lives: an unstoppable force we can only embrace and work with, not against. Sudden encounters and news from abroad should always be expected whenever this card shows up. In contrast to the Tower though, the Eight of Wands shows us that we have everything we need to navigate this change and make the situation work in our favor.

But the Eight of Wands can also be a warning against making too hasty decisions. When faced with a changing situation, are we perhaps reacting too spasmodically and losing our aim and focus? Even the most powerful arrow throw is useless if it is not aimed toward a specific target.

Nine of Wands

An injured soldier is holding on to his wand like a staff. Eight more wands are towering behind him and the soldier, looking weary and tattered, is glancing at them suspiciously. The tight belt around his waist representing his tight resolve, the man may be exhausted but he doesn't seem ready to give up. Maintaining an alert position, he understands that there may be another upcoming battle to fight, but perhaps that battle will be the last one.

The Nine of Wands brings us mixed messages: we are tired from our efforts, but hopeful that the attainment of our goal is in sight.

Like the soldier, we too have come a long way and achieved a lot, very often at a big personal cost. So now that we are called to prove our worth once again, be it at work or at another creative endeavor we feel passionate about, we feel somewhat fed up. But we know we've come a very long way to give up now.

However the Nine of Wands can be a sign that our insecurity and paranoia are getting the best of us. Contrary to what we may be feeling right now, not all our colleagues or peers are "out to get us". Is our exhaustion making us see enemies that are not actually there?

Ten of Wands

Ten Wands are being carried by a man, who seems to be really struggling under their weight. Bundled together tightly, the wands are blocking the man's view: he is heading toward a village, a representation of reaping the rewards for his struggles, but he can't see how near or far the village actually is. All he can do is keep putting one foot in front of the other and trust he won't drop his precious bundle now that he's so close to completing his journey.

Like all the suit cards with the number 10, the Ten of Wands indicates completion. We have reached the end of a circle. We have achieved our goals — although perhaps we are too preoccupied by the many responsibilities that came with them, to be able to relax and take stock of our gains.

Ten of Wands also acts as a warning: have we taken on too much, risking a burnout along the way? Wouldn't things be much simpler if we just delegated our efforts and let others help us with the workload? Sometimes, sharing our success may be the only way to achieve it.

Page of Wands

Standing on a barren land, a yound and finely dressed man is holding a wand with both hands. He is focusing his gaze on the subtle growth of leaves at the wand's tip, the only source of fertile nature visible, representing the spark of new ideas and budding new interests in a world that perhaps is not ready for them yet. The man's golden hair are a symbol of his intelligence whereas the salamanders adorning his shirt signify transformation. He is on the cusp of discovering something magnificent and telling everyone about it.

Page of Wands speaks to our inner child, the one who is brimming with enthusiam while taking on a new hobby or when meeting a new person. Like the young man in the card, we too want to share our newfound interests with the world, but it currently seems like there is nobody around who would be interested in hearing us. Thankfully, the lack of audience doesn't dim our joy.

But the Page of Wands can also be a bit too restless and spontaneous for its own good. Are we starting too many new projects but failing to invest the time and seriousness needed to see them through to the end?

Knight of Wands

Riding on his orange horse, a symbol for his fiery nature, the Knight of Wands is determined and ready for action. The shirt over his glossy armor has the same salamander patter with the Page of Wands to indicate transformation — only here it seems a bit tattered at the end, a symbol of the Knight's bigger life experience compared to the Page. Holding his wand with one hand and his horse's reins with the other, the Knight of Wands is ready to jump to reach his destination faster. The mane of his helmet brings to mind flames, signifying his passion and urgency.

The Knight of Wands urges us to be bold and not hesitate. To "fall head over heels", whether it is for a new romantic interest, a new job or a new creative endeavor. No half measures will do, only fierce determination and going all in. The Knight of Wands is also an auspicious card when it comes to travel, new adventures and new beginnings in general.

But as the Knight of Wands can also come off as a bit too hot-headed, so can we, while caught up in our own storm, make mistakes of judgement or accidentally hurt the feelings of people around us. Can we temper our passion with the voice of reason to avoid falling headfirst into a blunder?

Queen of Wands

The Queen of Wands is sitting on her throne, adorned with symbols of pride, passion and happiness: lions, flames and sunflowers. She is holding a wand on her right hand and a sunflower on the other, balancing her more nurturing nature and her great intuition with her assertiveness, her rational thought and her ability to lead. A black cat sitting at her feet, hints to the fact that the Queen of Wands, although sweet and warm, can become a dangerous opponent if you cross her.

Like the Queen of Wands, we too are called to combine all the different aspects of our personality if we want to live our best life. Usually representing a female ally coming to our aid, to help us with a work-related or even a personal issue, the Queen of Wands can also represent our own inner female energy, who knows that beauty and intelligence are complementary forces, not mutually exclusive.

But the Queen of Wands can also serve as a warning that we have become too self-absorbed. Are we caught in the beauty of our own reflections and failing to face some of our flaws?

King of Wands

Gazing thoughtfully in the distance, the King of Wands sits on his throne. His long cloak, like the tapestry on his throne, is adorned with lions and salamanders that are biting their tails — symbols of infinity, transformation, strength and the ability to surpass obstacles. A small, live salamander rests safely at his feet, a hint at f the King's protective nature. On his fiery red hair, a golden crown shaped like flames represents passion and wisdom. The King of Wands is holding his staff with his right hand, while the left is resting calmly on his lap, signifying that he rules with effortless power.

The King of Wands usually represents a male mentor figure in our lives, there to help and guide us through professional and creative challenges. Combining bravery and determination with the wisdom of experience, the King of Wands is also our inner teacher: the accomplished part of ourselves who wants to spread his knowledge and help others.

But the King of Wands can also be overbearing and arrogant at times. Absolute power, even tempered with wisdom, can make us believe that we know what's best for people. Can we keep our ego in check while we help others flourish?

Cups

The last suit is the Cups suit. Associated with Autumn and with the element of Water, this suit is all about our emotional world: our powers of intuition, our need for romance, friendship, commitment, flirting and a happy ending.

Ace of Cups

Emerging from a cloud amid a grey, yet calm sky, an aetherial hand surrounded by a halo is holding the Ace of Cups like an offering. Overflowing with water representing emotional fulfillment and creativity, the Ace of Cups stands above a serene pond filled with lotus blossoms, a symbol of spiritual awakening and openness. A dove, carrying a wafer on its beak about to place it inside the Ace of Cups, signifies the Holy Communion and a a bestowal of blessings from above. Five streams of water running from the cup represent our five senses, uniting the spiritual with the physical realm.

As the aetherial hand seems to be offering the Ace of Cups, so are we being offered an opportunity for emotional rebirth. A sign that our feelings are being reciprocated or that a new relationship or creative project is on the horizon, the Ace of Cups is an inherently positive card. It's time to drink from the cup of life.

But the Ace of Cups can also imply a tendency to ignore our rational mind and make choices based only on our emotions. Can we be objective when faced with matters of the heart?

Two of Cups

Sheltered underneath the wings of the red alchemical lion, a representation of the attraction and harmonious coexistence of volatile forces, a man and a woman are offering the Two of Cups to one another. Gazing intently into their loved one's eyes, the couple is wearing wreaths on their hair, a symbol of their many achievements in life and the strength they each are bringing into this union. They are raising the Two of Cups in opposite hands, balancing the male and female energies, while the staff of Hermes between them signifies duality and good health. The couple clearly has the protection of cosmic forces and they are headed toward a happy life, on the little house on the hill.

The Two of Cups invites us to toast to a new relationship or partnership. Although predominantly a card that signifies our mutual decision to commit to our romantic partner, the Two of Cups is also a great sign for any kind of contract or agreement we are currently working on solidifying. When we find the perfect partner (romantic, platonic or professional), we become stronger together.

But the Two of Cups can be a warning that we tend to over-glorify our relationships. Are we glossing over potential problems in order to convince ourselves and the world that we have met our perfect someone?

Three of Cups

Three women, symbolizing the three Greek goddesses of charisma (Graces), are raising the Three of Cups while dancing under a radiant blue sky. The bearers of the Three of Cups, their long robes suggesting inner radiance, success and zest for life, are all crowned with wreaths and there is a plentiful harvest underneath their feet. Their hands are interconnected, a mark of their strong and harmonious bond, while one of the women is also holding grapes

— an indication that these are clearly bountiful times, worthy of celebration.

A reminder to embrace the things that bring us joy, the Three of Cups invites us to unleash our inner Grace. On a more practical level, the Three of Cups speaks of all the exhilarating moments spent in the presence of good friends and enjoyable company. A party, birthday celebration or even a wedding may be in our near future when this card appears.

The Three of Cups however can be a warning that we have been oversharing, or relying too much to our friends and support system. Could we stand on our own and still radiate joy without being followed by our entourage?

Four of Cups

Under a sycamore tree, a man is sitting with his arms and legs crossed, a symbol of inertia and separation from the world around him. Appearing deep in contemplation, the man does not seem to notice or care about the lush green hill he is sitting on, or the gold cup presented to him by an aetherial hand emerging from a cloud. Three more gold cups on his feet represent all the things he has achieved or possesses already, and yet he fails to feel enthusiastic about.

The Four of Cups is a sign we don't quite feel content with how our life is currently unraveling. Although we may at first glance have everything we could possibly desire, there is an inner disconnect and an inability to accept life's many blessings. Just like the man depicted in the card, so are we being presented with an opportunity to chance our current situation for the better... if only we come out of our bubble, stop taking our blessings for granted and really look around us.

But the Four of Cups is also a warning that greed will get us nowhere. Do we constantly yearn for more in order to feel satisfied?

Five of Cups

A man wrapped in a black cloak, a symbol of loss and despair, is standing inconsolable near a river that flows incessantly, like the flow of emotions. With his body turned toward the water, the man does not seem to acknowledge all of the Five of Cups surrounding him. Three of the cups are emptied in front of him, their contents spilled on the ground as an allegory for emotional loss and suffering, but two cups are still standing behind the man — a symbol that the situation may not be as dire as he chooses to believe. At the far end, a bridge is promising to take the man away from this destitute situation and into a more positive place.

The Five of Cups may at first glance convey sadness and disappointment, but the card's true message is to stop focusing on what has been lost and be grateful for everything that is "still standing" in our lives. Only through a mentality shift that will allows to accept what we cannot change, can we move forward to bigger and better things.

The Five of Cups can also speak of a tendency to blame ourselves for situations that couldn't possibly have been within our control. Should we keep trying to punish ourselves for our perceived failings?

Six of Cups

Playing outside a castle, a symbol of comfort and security further accentuated by the presence of the guard in the back, two children are surrounded by the Six of Cups. Each cup is filled to the brim with verdant greens and white flowers, representing vitality and innocence. The boy, dressed in red and blue to convey his zest for life and inner calmness, is giving one of the cups to the little girl, as a token of friendship and appreciation. The girl is accepting the cup with white gloves in her hands, a further mark of innocence and purity.

The Six of Cups is a card of happy reunions and nostalgic trips down memory lane. Whether it speaks of meeting old friends or of rediscovering our inner playfulness, Six of Cups reminds us that it is important to look at the world through the wide, full of amazement eyes of a child.

But the Six of Cups can also imply a reluctance to "grow up" and change our habits. Are we so attached to how things and relationships used to be that we cannot see the positive aspects of starting something new?

Seven of Cups

Seven of Cups emerge from a cloud, bringers of a phantasmagoria that complete overshadows the man who is gazing at them. A different spectre is emerging from each cup: a human head or mask, for the man's public persona or potential partnership; a phantom, for the need to unveil the man's true spiritual self; a snake, for sexuality, knowledge and change; a tower, for security and stability; shiny jewels, for wealth; a laurel wreath, for victory and pride; a dragon, for the man's inner darkness. The man seems unable to choose which cup to pick, lost in the fantasies and illusions each choice represents.

The Seven of Cups is an indication that we are currently searching for purpose. Perhaps we are being presented with many choices, but neither of them is exactly right for us. If a situation or a person appears too good to be true, we need to consider whether perhaps they are.

The Seven of Cups also warns us: having an active fantasy is not a bad thing, but getting lost in daydreams about how things could potentially turn out, will get us nowhere. Has our head been stuck in the clouds for too long?

Eight of Cups

During a moonlit night, a cloaked figure is seen walking away from the Eight of Cups. In contrast to the Five of Cups though, this time the man's cloak is red — a symbol of determination and of the man's adamant belief something more exciting is waiting for him down the road. He has already crossed the river from where the Eight of Cups lie, signifying that his emotional detachment from the current situation has already begun. The Moon, representing the need to listen to one's intuition, seems to be looking down at the man who has a long and arduous journey in front of him.

The Eight of Cups is a sign that we are ready to embark on a path of personal growth and leave what no longer serves us behind. From ending a relationship or a work partnership to moving to a different appartment or simply quitting a habit that was bad for us, the Eight of Cups promises that change may be hard, but it will be worth it.

But the Eight of Cups can also be a warning we may be leaving behind things or people that are important to us, simply out of boredom. Are we being too quick to abandon ship?

Nine of Cups

A clearly rich man, wearing a red hat that represents his ambition and drive, is sitting on an ornate bench in front of a shelf where the Nine of Cups are being displayed. His arms crossed across his chest, the man's body language and self-contented face expression seem to convey pride of his achievements and a determination to maintain them. The blue cloth underneath the Nine of Cups symbolizes the man's inner calmness but also his conviction that he deserves everything he has gained.

The Nine of Cups is a sign that we will probably be getting what we wanted — whether it's material possessions or a fortuitous development in some area of our lives. Also called the "wish card", the Nine of Cups shows us that happiness is possible not just to attain, but to maintain as well. We need to have confidence, in ourselves and in the Universe.

But the Nine of Cups reminds us that in order to get what we really want, we should first be honest with ourselves about what that is. Should we be more careful what we wish for?

Ten of Cups

Framed by a halo and a radiant rainbow, a symbol of divine blessings and favorable circumstances, the Ten of Cups are floating in the sky. Underneath them, a happy couple are sharing an embrace, their hands held high as if saluting the beautiful day. Dressed in red and blue representing passion and emotional stability, the couple is clearly at that stage where their relationship is tested and true. Next to them, two children are playing, their clothes mirroring those of their parents. The lush, green scenery in front of them represents prosperity and happiness; a life that's nurtured by positive emotions the same way the trees are nurtured by the water of the stream.

Ten of Cups is one of the most positive cards to come across. We are surrounded by love and have achieved harmony in our relationships. A great card for marriage, having children or buying a house together, the Ten of Cups can also symbolize reaping the rewards of our efforts and basking in the appreciation of our community.

The Ten of Cups though can sometimes be an indication we are working hard to maintain this flawless facade in our relationship or marriage. Have we become obsessed with our pursuit of perfection?

Page of Cups

His back to the sea, the Page of Cups is inspecting the fish he has caught in his golden cup. The young man is dressed in pink and blue, representing a balance between his feminine, intuitive side, and his masculine, rational side. The lotus flowers on the Page of Cups represent his spiritual awakening, while the fish he caught on the cup symbolizes the birth of a new creative idea, endeavor or even a "hunch" the Page has — but is unsure what to do with it yet.

Just like the Page of Cups, so may we be feeling suddenly inspired and yet unsure what to do with our inspiration. This card is an invitation to nurture our creativity and try our hand in something new, perhaps an art-related hobby. A new flirt may appear in the horizon as well, and the Page of Cups reminds us to be sweet but also reasonable about it. It's not the time to fall head over heels yet, but it may be soon.

The Page of Cups can also serve as a warning of coming off as overly sensitive and childish. Do we really enjoy being perceived as the fragile flower?

Knight of Cups

His horse halting before crossing a stream, the Knight of Cups is holding a golden cup like a message to be delivered. Making his way forward slowly but elegantly on what seems to be a foreign land, the Knight of Cups features wings on his helmet and feet, a clear sign of his communication and diplomacy skills but also of his mercurial nature. Worn over his armour, the Knight's cloak is adorned with fish and running waters, representing intuition and inspiration, the red color an indication of this Knight's passion, idealism and charisma.

The Knight of Cups usually represents an offer we can't refuse, made by a very charming individual. Whether it's an invitation to a party, being asked out on a date or a professional opportunity, something exciting is definitely coming in the horizon. The Knight of Cups can also represent the progress we are making in our artistic endeavors: we're ready to share our work of art with the world.

But for all his charm, the Knight of Cups may not always be sincere. Are we being fooled by pretty words and failing to see the intentions behind them?

Queen of Cups

Her ornate throne placed right at the intersection of ocean and land to represent the different realms of emotion and reason, the Queen of Cups seems to be preoccupied by the trophy she holds. It's a cup, but closed (a nod to the subconscious) and adorned with religious symbols and two angels that seem to be guarding it on each side. Small mermaid children carved on her throne depict the Queen of Cups' motherly nature and giving soul, but also her potential for being overly dramatic and unpredictable. Her feet, dressed in blue slippers to signify calm emotions, do not touch the water: she is in control.

The Queen of Cups has been characterized many times as the "drama queen" of the Minor Arcana, but this is not always the case. This card invites us to pay attention to our emotions and intuitions, the deep reasons that are making us behave a certain way. We should not discount the messages our subconscious is trying to deliver: it is our intuitive nature that will set us apart and help us excel at a project or creative endeavor.

The Queen of Cups though is ultimately a card of emotions — and no matter how hard we try, we can't always keep them in check. Are we becoming blinded by them?

King of Cups

Whereas the Queen of Cups' throne was just on the ocean's shore, the King of Cups reigns right above it — but his feet, resting on his concrete throne, are never touching the water. Holding a golden cup in his right hand and a golden wand in his left, the King of Cups represents balance between the yin and yang qualities of assertiveness and acceptance. A fish-shaped necklace marks the King's creative personality, while the red details on his crown and cloak are a symbol of his power and ability to discern and make the most out of opportunities, further signified by the boat approaching behind him.

The King of Cups is a benevolent and generous ruler, who reminds us to always give first in order to receive. When this card appears, it may be an indication that we need to be diplomatic and not act based on our emotions alone, in order to secure success. The King of Cups may also symbolize a mentor, usually male, who can help us attain perfection in a project or endeavor.

The King of Cups however, especially in a love reading, can also represent a partner who is being a bit cold and reserved — or our own tendency to not show our emotions. Can we try wearing our heart a bit more on our sleeve?

CREATE YOUR OWN RULES AND RITUALS

You now hold the secrets of the tarot cards in your hands, dear one. Use them wisely. Understand your tools and their power — but also understand that power, ultimately, lies within.

For example: based on the type of tarot card reading you want to do, you'll find thousands of tarot spreads out there, some as simple as 3-card spreads, other as complicated as 15-card spreads. Don't be tempted to go for the complicated right away. Your intuition will work much better if you don't suffocate it with a barrage of images as you draw card after card after card.

Start small.

Begin by establishing a connection with your deck; it's a valuable tool and a partner in your work, so treat it with respect. Cleanse it with palo santo or sage, charge it with a selenite or a rose quartz crystal and make sure it's always dust-free. Light a candle, say a prayer to your matron deities, give thanks for the answers you will receive. And then, don't worry so much about what kind of spread you need to do: just pull a few cards that feel "right".

In general, you'll notice that as you're getting started on your divination techniques (and falling in love with the process) the temptation to add more elements, theatricality and well, props, will be immense. There are simply too many cute tarot cloths out there!

But at the end of the day, you don't need anything else but yourself, your intuition and the Goddess. If your intuition tells you to also draw a rune to clarify a tarot reading, go for it, no one will mind. If your intuition tells you to throw your cards on the floor like dice and see what comes up (or have your cat pick a card for you) then by all means dear one, go ahead.

The future is in your hands. It always has been.

Chapter 4: Seasonal Spells

We've already seen how Pagans love to celebrate — and thankfully, the Wheel of the Year offers many opportunities for merrymaking!

In this chapter, we'll go through the major Wiccan Sabbats and Esbats and discuss the kind of energies that are present during each one, as well as some tips for seasonal spellcasting!

Are you ready, dear one?

Samhain

Also called "a Witch's New Year", Samhain kickstarts the magickal Wheel of the Year. Celebrated on the eve of October 31, Samhain was one of the biggest old Pagan rituals that Christianity repurposed as All Hallow's Night and we all now celebrate as Halloween[28]. On Samhain, the veil between the worlds is at its thinnest, with spirits crossing over — so it's ideal for divination, spells to reveal ancestors' secrets and spells of rebirth.

---

[28] Mandy Mitchell, (2014) Hedgewitch Book of Days: Spells, Rituals, and Recipes for the Magical Year, Weiser Books.

An easy Samhain spell to try is making an extra plate of food for a beloved one that has passed (can also be a pet). Set it on the table along with a black or purple candle and give thanks. If you're celebrating with your family, honor the memory of the dead — if you're alone, talk to them. Once your dinner is done, take the offered plate outside and leave it for the spirits (a great idea to also leave a lantern alight all night long). Return to the table, with the candle still burning, and taking out your tarot cards (or your prefered divination method), ask the spirit of your beloved for guidance. Closing your eyes, let your hands be guided towards the right cards or runes to gleam their answers.

YULE

We've already discussed how Yule was celebrated in the Old Norse tradition and many of its Pagan customs have now become a part of Christmas. Yule falls around December 21, on the night of the winter solstice, the longest night of the year. Honor the Pagan traditions by gathering the whole family for a meal, let the Yule Log burn all night long (someone should take turns looking at it all night to make sure it doesn't go out) and hang mistletoe, the sacred plant of the Druids and associated with Freya, on your doorstep.

Yule is more of a time for celebration than it is a time for spellcasting. But there is one simple candle spell you can try: take a golden candle (to represent the birth of the Sun) and carve symbols with your athame to represent the things you want to awaken in your own life. The symbols can be as simple as a heart for love, or as complicated as the alchemical symbol for earth, to symbolize abundance — it's really up to you! Light your candle and sprinkle a pinch of cinnamon while it burns, for success on your endeavors. Chant four times:

"In this, the year's longest night,

light up the spark of new delight,

to the darkness shed some light"

Imbolc

Also known as Brighid's Day, celebrated on February 2, Imbolc is the time when Spring slowly starts awakening. This is actually a great time to dedicate yourself to your Craft: go out in the woods and see if you can find a branch to turn into yout wand; decorate your Book of Shadows and start using it; teach yourself to read the runes. Brighid loved poetry and writing, so try writing a magickal poem that contains the things you want to awaken in your life this Springtime. You can also make a wicker doll in her honor.

Candle magick is often used in Imbolc — choose a pale blue color candle and carve with your athame symbols of what you want to manifest. Do it in runes, to better appease Bridgid.

It's also a great idea to plant some bulbs in indoor pots, imbuing them with the intention of the things you want to bloom in your life.

Ostara

Celebrated around March 21, Ostara officially marks the return of the Sun. It's one of those Pagan festivals that have been repurposed by Christianity, so you won't have trouble finding decorations for it: Ostara decorations are actually all about bunnies, little chicks and paste-colored eggs! (And yes, Ostara is where the word Easter comes from.) Feel free to paint eggs yourself, in the colors of the energies you want to bring into your life.

Ribbon magick is great for this Sabbat: pick ribbons in colors that symbolize the things you want to bring, change or manifest (green for wealth, yellow for happiness and creativity, pink for love etc) and after you purify them and imbue them with energy from the

Elements, particularly Air, make knots on them and hang them from trees (or from your doorway if you're living in an urban apartment). As you tie them, chant:

"One knot to bring wishes my way

Two to be kind and let them stay

Three, four and five to open my door

Six to usher them in for evermore"

BELTANE

Ah, Beltane! It's the second most important Pagan festival after Samhain — and its antithesis. Celebrated on May 1, Beltane is a feast of life, lust and sexuality. (Remember that maypole people used to dance around in villages of old?)

The best thing you can do in Beltane to be honest is drink and dance with friends, and find someone special to flirt with. Love spells are particularly strong around this time of year but only perform them to attract loving energy in your life, not a particular person (because bewitching someone to show interest in you goes against the Wiccan Law).

An easy and Wiccan-friendly love spell is to fill your chalice with wine (doesn't matter what kind, choose the one you love the flavor of), two strawberries, a sprig of basil and a pink quartz crystal. If you have a tarot card deck, you can also pick the Two of Cups card and place it under or next to your chalice. Leave it the glass near a windowsill, preferably somewhere where the moonlight can access it. On Beltane day, preferably before going out to party, pick out the strawberries and eat them slowly, consuming the loving energy. You can opt to drink the wine or spill it in the earth for your upcoming romance to root. Take the tarot card with you in your wallet.

Go out and have a magickal night!

LITHA

Also known as Midsummer, Litha, the Summer Solstice, is celebrated on June 21st. Much like Yule, Litha is a time for celebration and eating out with friends, lighting bonfires and spend the day at the beach or near trees — leave the serious spellcasting for other Sabbats. That being said, Litha is ideal for flower magick.

Pick the flowers that symbolize the things you want to bring more of in your life (for instance, roses for passion, marigolds for happiness and marriage) and turn them into a flower crown that you'll wear for the day. And before you go to bed at night, leave a glass of milk outside for the fairies, to make sure your wishes are granted. Shakespear knew a thing or two when he wrote about fairies in Midsummer Night's Dream.

LAMMAS

Celebrated on August 1, Lammas (also known as Lughhasadh) is a harvest festival dedicated to the Sun and to the god Lugh. This is a great Sabbat to awaken your inner Kitchen Witch and bake a loaf of magickal bread. The recipe you'll use for the bread doesn't matter, as long as you knead it by hand, manifesting your intentions with every movement. You can also use your athame to carve symbols on the loaf before you put it in the oven. Chant:

"Golden loaf of sun's reward

Bake my wishes as foretold"

Once the bread is out of the oven, still warm, take a piece with your right hand and eat it. You can accompany it with a glass of beer to further celebrate this Harvest.

Mabon

The second harvest festival, Mabon, is celebrated around September 21 on the autumn equinox. Mabon symbolizes the balance between darkness and light: you should light one black and one white candle (or just one grey candle) during this Sabbat.

Apples and pomegranates are considered sacred fruit during Mabon and you would be wise to consume both on this day. Save some of the apple seeds for your altar, to give as an offering.

Chapter 5: Final Words of Warning

All magic comes with a price. Isn't that what you see people saying in every fictional show or movie whenever anybody performs a spell?

"Price" may not be the right word for it. "Balancing act" is probably more accurate.

You see, dear one, every time you perform a spell or do a ritual, the ones you read in this book or others you will create and finetune on your own, you invoke a certain amount of Power. That Power may come from within you, and often does (although it's not recommended because then you're left completely drained and exhausted most of the time) but usually it is at least amplified, if not emanating, from the Elements, the Energies and the Deities you invoke.

You are taking something from this world, to shape it into something of your choosing and create something else. And because Nature hates a vacuum (scientists would agree to that) something else must be created to take its place.

Our world is not perfectly balanced as this above paragraph implies, that's true. Many times, balance takes a while to be restored — you may not even feel its repercussions in your lifetime. But restored it will be, eventually.

"Mind the Three-fold Laws you should three times bad and three times good."

This verse from the Wiccan Rede[29] describes in no uncertain terms that whatever energy you put out there, it comes back to you three times.

As we've seen, the Wiccan Rede is a Neopaganistic poem composed in the '60s to create some kind of a common code for the Wiccans — and the Three-fold Law is integral to it, as it is the

---

[29] "The Wiccan Rede" (Full Version) as depicted in The Celtic Connection website, https://wicca.com/celtic/wicca/rede.htm

"An harm none, do as thou will" position. But the notion of getting back what you give is certainly not a novel one. Karma is a similar idea; the Hinduistic and Buddhist belief that one's actions and intentions shape one's future. Hinduism in particular has some other concepts similar to the idea of the Three-fold Law: Sanchita, Vartamana and Prarabdha, which talk about your accumulated works, your current work and your future endeavors as part of one chain of events.

Or, in plain English: who you've been influences who you are which influences who you'll become. It makes sense, doesn't it?

As for the "three times" part, we need to take into consideration how sacred the number three is to Wiccans, denoting the triple aspect of the Goddess as Maiden, Mother and Crone. Plus, the people who wrote the Wiccan Rede wanted to emphasize the importance of kindness and of doing good work, so getting three times more good things than you put out there sounds more motivational than saying "what you give is exactly what you get".

If you are a Wiccan, of if you beginning to identify as one now that you've read this book, then I probably don't have to try any harder to convince you to follow this rule. If you are not though, or if this book made you realize you identify more with Pagans and/or Witches than you do with Wiccans, I need you to consider this very carefully.

You believe that you can co-create your reality, right? If you didn't, you wouldn't have gotten this far in this book. You believe that your intentions can shape your life and you can put out there the energies you want to put out there in order to live your life as you want it… right? Then ask yourself, dear one: if what you're putting out there is darkness (and not the Sacred kind), if what you're putting out there is ego and negativity, what do you think will fill your life?

We are what we do most often.

You may swear you're a good person until the cows come home, but if at the end of the day you're intentionally using magic to hurt others or to give yourself an unfair advantage then you will, sooner or later, get what's coming to you.

Please don't consider this a threat. It's not I, the author of this book, who will punish you for misusing magic. This book is not cursed. On the contrary, I've imbued it with only blessings and good wishes for you, to guide you in your journey (wherever that journey may take you). What I'm trying to say is that when you open yourself to negative energies, the negative energies listen. And they usually come — and bring some friends, in the form of unclean or restless spirits, with them.

Oh, they will entice you at first, make you feel powerful... that's how they operate. And then, they will convince you that you need them: that you need to accumulate more power or more of that thing you're currently after (Money? Attention? Affection?). After a while, even "more" won't be enough to really fill your soul. You'll get trapped in your own belief you can do everything and you'll keep tapping into your energy resources until you deplete them. Or, you'll keep serving these bad energies all your life (some people do) and then, when it's time to leave this realm for your next cycle of rebirth, you won't have learned anything. You'll probably have to be reborn under harsher circumstances, so that you can learn different lessons than last time.

That is not cruelty. It's not punishment or "paying the price". It is simply, unequivocally, Balance.

But it is this author's hope that you understand all this already. It is this author's hope that you've come into all this with good intentions, and you're leaving with even better ones. It is this author's hope that you'll use the things you learned in this book to make your life and the life of other beings (to the best of your abilities, of course) as full and radiant as possible.

It is this author's hope that you will be one with the Goddess, one with Nature and one with Yourself.

Be well, Pagans and Wiccan, Witches and Magicians.

Be kind, laugh often and make Magick. Always with a k.

BIBLIOGRAPHY

Bryant, Tamera (2005). The Life & Times of Hammurabi. Bear: Mitchell Lane Publishers.

Cameron, Alan G. (2011). The Last Pagans of Rome. New York: Oxford University Press.

Crowley, Aleister. The Equinox of the Gods. New Falcon Publications, 1991.

Cunningham, Scott, (1987), Cunningham's Encyclopedia of Crystal, Gem, and Metal Magic.

Cunningham, Scott, (1985) Cunningham's Encyclopedia of Magical Herbs.

Dixson, Alan F., and Barnaby Dixson. 2011. "Venus Figurines of the European Paleolithic: Symbols of Fertility or Attractiveness?" Journal of Anthropology 2011.

Doyle White, Ethan (2016). "Old Stones, New Rites: Contemporary Pagan Interactions with the Medway Megaliths". Material Religion: The Journal of Objects, Art and Belief.

Friberg, Eino; Landström, Björn; Schoolfield, George C., eds. (1988), The Kalevala: Epic of the Finnish People.

Gardner, Gerald (1954). Witchcraft Today. London: Rider.

Goscinny, René & Uderzo, Albert, (1963) Astérix et Cléopâtre, Pilote magazine.

Gaiman, Neil, (2017) Norse Mythology, Bloomsbury Publishing PLC.

Kazantzakis, Nikos. At the Palaces of Knossos. London: Owen, 1988.

Kramer, Heinrich & Sprenger, Jacob, (1486) Malleus Maleficarum, translated by Montague Summers, 2011, Martino Fine Books.

Leland, Charles Godfrey (1899). Aradia, or the Gospel of the Witches. David Nutt.

Medhurst, W. H. Ancient China. The Shoo King or the Historical Classic. Shanghai: The Mission Press.

Mitchell, Mandy, (2014) Hedgewitch Book of Days: Spells, Rituals, and Recipes for the Magical Year, Weiser Books.

Murray, Margaret A. (1921). The Witch-Cult in Western Europe. Oxford: Clarendon Press.

Murray, Margaret A. (1931). The God of the Witches. London: Faber and Faber.

Old Testament: The Book of Genesis.

Ruickbie, Leo, Witchcraft Out of the Shadows: A Complete History, Robert Hale; New edition (April 1, 2012).

Runyon, Carroll (1997). Secrets of the Golden Dawn Cipher Manuscripts. C.H.S.

Valiente, Doreen (1989). The Rebirth of Witchcraft. London: Robert Hale.

Walsh, William, (1970) The Story of Santa Klaus, Gale Research Company.

Yates, Frances A., Giordano Bruno and the Hermetic Tradition. University of Chicago Press, 1964.

The Complete I Ching - 10th Anniversary Edition : The Definitive Translation by Taoist Master Alfred Huang, Inner Traditions Bear and Company.

Websites:

"The Wiccan Rede" (Full Version) as depicted in The Celtic Connection website, https://wicca.com/celtic/wicca/rede.htm

www.ingramcontent.com/pod-product-compliance
Lightning Source LLC
Chambersburg PA
CBHW071728080526
44588CB00013B/1938